Why Not?

Travel Odysseys of An Indian Passport, An Unstoppable Woman, Many Misunderstood Lands

By Ankitha Rajendaran

Printed in India

IndiePress

ISBN:

First Printing, 2025

IndiePress

A division of Nasadiya Technologies Private Ltd.

Koramangala, Bengaluru

Karnataka–560029

http://indiepress.in/

Edited by Ridham Bassi

Typeset by MAP Systems, Bengaluru

Book Cover designed by Sankhashubro Nath

Publishing Consultant: Rechal Fernandes

Table of Contents

PREFACE AND ABOUT THE AUTHOR

The Distance Between Here and There

What's the moment that makes you feel alive when you're far from home? Maybe it's the first bite of something so spicy your eyes water, but you can't stop eating. Or when a stranger with no reason to help smiles and says, "Come, I'll show you." For me, it's that electric jolt of realizing, *I don't know what's coming next, but I'm here for it.*

For me, travel has never been about the places I can plot on a map. It's about the unexpected—a street musician in Tehran playing a song that makes your chest ache, or a child in Rwanda sharing a laugh so pure it could outshine the sun. It's about realizing, over and over again, how little divides us and how much we share.

But let's be real: travel isn't always romantic montages and soul-stirring revelations. It's also sweat-soaked shirts, missed buses, and the kind of exhaustion that makes you question every life choice. And yet, in those clumsy, impromptu moments, I've found something far more valuable than picture-perfect postcards—a deeper sense of who I am. In between the bad coffee and language fails, you also stumble across something real—people who remind you why the world is so damn beautiful.

This isn't a book about getting it "right." I'm not here to give you advice on chasing sunsets or finding the best hole-in-the-wall cafes. Instead, it's about how travel shifts the ground beneath your feet, showing you what really matters: courage, connection, and the stories you didn't even know you were carrying.

As you turn these pages, I hope you'll feel more than inspired; I hope you'll feel seen. Because this isn't just about where I've been; it's about what happens when we all step out of our own way and let the world surprise us. So, here's the deal. Forget your bucket list for a second. Forget the glossy travel blogs and "must-see" lists. Let's talk about the kind of journey that stays with you long after your passport's tucked away. That's what I've discovered here, and I hope you will too.

The Universe's Favorite Child

I've often joked that I must be the universe's favorite child. It started as a lighthearted quip to explain my knack for finding myself surrounded by incredible people—family, friends, strangers-turned-guides—who've lifted me, shielded me, and opened paths I never thought possible. Over time, though, that joke has turned into something more profound:

a belief that luck, faith, and human connection have been the invisible scaffolding of my life.

From the outside, I know it's easy to mistake me for someone who never falters. People sometimes see my confidence and assume I've always been sure of myself, that I've walked through life immune to the fears and uncertainties that others carry. But nothing could be further from the truth. My story, like anyone's, is woven with vulnerability—not as a flaw, but as the very thing that makes me who I am.

A Foundation of Freedom

Growing up as a third-culture child—Indian by heritage, raised in Oman, educated in the U.S., and now living in Dubai—I learned early on to embrace a world without fixed borders. My upbringing was a mosaic of experiences, each piece challenging me to see the world as interconnected rather than divided. My home was filled with lively debates about politics, gender, and culture, often led by my mother, a feminist in every sense of the word. She wasn't content to let the world dictate its terms to her; she questioned, challenged, and shared her opinions freely. My father, her equal in every way, championed her voice and encouraged mine.

Together, they created a home where individuality wasn't just accepted but celebrated. My mother taught me the power of opinion, and my father gave me the freedom to act on it. It was my father who told me, time and again, that the world was mine to explore. His words weren't just encouragement; they were permission to dream as boldly as

I wanted. That freedom became the cornerstone of my life. I've never been someone to fit neatly into boxes or conform to expectations. My parents didn't raise me to be defined by societal norms—they raised me to define myself.

How I Met Anand

Somewhere along the way, life threw me a wild card named Anand. We met in college in Chennai, back in 2009 when we were both undergrads. What began as campus banter turned into a love story that has spanned continents, long-distance calls, and countless shared adventures.

Our relationship wasn't without its challenges. For three and a half years, we navigated a long-distance relationship that tested our patience and resolve. But love, it seems, has a way of bridging even the widest oceans. After reconnecting in the U.S. during our MBA days, we tied the knot in 2013. We were just 24—young, ambitious, and ready to grow together as partners.

Fifteen years later, we're still figuring it out—still balancing our individual dreams with our shared journey. Anand is, as I often describe him, my yin. Where I charge ahead, he carefully maps the terrain. Where I embrace risk, he weighs consequences. Our differences are the glue that holds us together.

The Feminist Men in My Life

Let's start with the feminist men. Yes, feminist men—a phrase that feels unusual but perfectly describes the men who've been pivotal in my life. If my upbringing taught me to embrace individuality, the men in my life have shown me what true partnership looks like. My father, my brother, my husband, my boss—each of them has shaped me in ways I couldn't have imagined.

My father, for example, has always been my north star. Perseverance, clarity of thought, and commitment to one's principles are values I learned from him. But more importantly, he gave me wings to fly. His pride in my independence was never conditional, never tied to whether I followed a path others might expect.

Then there's my boss. Working with someone who believes in your vision is a gift, but my boss takes it a step further. He champions my journey rather than merely supporting it. He shares my travel stories with others more than I do myself, highlighting my adventures in rooms I haven't even entered. His belief in my work and his pride in my accomplishments have been invaluable in a world where professional environments can often stifle individuality.

Then there's my husband, a man who redefines partnership. Despite the fact that his profession would have flourished in the U.S., he traversed continents with me since I did not want to stay there. I remember the conversation: I worried about finding a job while he had every opportunity lined up. But he said, "You're not going to compromise on what you want. Let's move." And we did. Even in the early days of our marriage, when I earned more than him, there was no ego, no discomfort—just pride and support. He's the kind of partner who says, "If you want to lead, I'll follow." His upbringing might have been traditional, but his mindset is beautifully progressive. And when you meet him, you'll see—it's not performative. It's just who he is.

My brother shares the same ethos, and even my boss has been a constant cheerleader, proudly sharing my journey with others more than I ever would. These men, along with my maternal grandfather—a man who valued education and progress above all—have shown me that feminism isn't confined to gender. It's a belief in the power of people to uplift each other, no matter their role or relationship.

The Women Who Raised Me

If my father gave me wings, my mother taught me how to soar. She's my best friend, my confidante, and one of the fiercest feminists I know. Growing up, I never saw a world of rigid gender roles in my home. My mother, often the sharpest mind in the room, voiced her opinions freely, and I watched my father respect and value them. That dynamic shaped how I see relationships—as partnerships of equals, where each person's voice matters.

My mother and I share adventures and not just a bond. I once took her to Africa, and we got stuck in a cyclone in Malawi. I still remember her calm confidence: "I know you'll get us home." And I did. That's the kind of faith she has in me—a faith that has fueled my belief in myself through the toughest challenges.

On Opinions, Politics, and Growing into Myself

As a child, politics, and world affairs were like distant mountains—visible but out of reach. Growing up in Oman, my worldview was shaped by the bubble of neutrality around me. But traveling changes you. It forces you to confront the narratives you were raised on and reevaluate them in the face of new realities.

When I visit countries like Syria, Afghanistan, and Iraq, I see firsthand the human cost of decisions made far from these lands. I've walked through homes destroyed by war, listened to people who've rebuilt their lives from nothing, and witnessed resilience in its rawest form. These experiences have given me a seat at the table, a voice rooted in credibility and firsthand understanding. That voice, however, didn't appear overnight. I've always had opinions, but now I speak with the confidence of someone who has seen the complexities of the world up close. And the feminist men in my life have always championed that voice.

Faith in Humanity

The truth is, I owe much of my journey to the kindness of strangers. In nations often labeled as "dangerous," I've depended on guides—people I had never met before—who have come through for me in ways that restored my faith in humanity.

It's a strange paradox, putting your life in the hands of people the world tells you to fear. But time and again, I've found that these individuals—show up with a generosity and courage that defy stereotypes. In those moments, I've felt the universe watching over me. Maybe it's luck, maybe it's karma, or maybe it's the power of believing in the goodness of people. Either way, these experiences have reinforced my belief that vulnerability isn't weakness—it's a doorway to connection.

Why Vulnerability Matters

Many mistake my fierceness for a lack of vulnerability. I've been told I come across as intimidating, as someone too confident or too unshaken to understand the fears and uncertainties of others. But vulnerability runs through every fiber of my story, every journey I've taken, and every challenge I've faced.

Here's the truth: vulnerability doesn't mean walking into situations unprepared or naive. It means recognizing that no matter how well you plan, the world will always surprise you. It means acknowledging that fear, uncertainty, and failure are inevitable, and that's okay. Vulnerability is what makes us human—it's the soil where resilience grows.

Each trip I've taken has been studded with moments of vulnerability. Whether it was navigating a cyclone with my mother, trusting a guide in a war zone, or watching immigration officers examine my passport with skepticism, I've felt the sting of uncertainty. But those moments have shaped me. They've taught me that fear doesn't define us; how we rise above it does. Vulnerability, in its rawest form, isn't about weakness—it's about being open to the unknown and trusting yourself to navigate it.

So, as you read this book, you'll find a story not of invincibility but of adaptation. You'll see how vulnerability has been my greatest teacher rather than an adversary. And if there's one lesson I hope to share, it's this: your vulnerability is not something to hide. It's something to embrace, for it's in those fragile moments that we truly discover our strength.

The Power of Vulnerability

What many people don't see, though, is the vulnerability that runs through my life and my travels. They see the woman who's been to 104 countries, who's walked through war zones and jungles, and they assume I'm fearless. But the truth is, vulnerability is the foundation of everything I've accomplished.

It is trusting a guide you've just met in a country the world has labeled "dangerous;" It's handing over your passport at a border crossing and waiting, heart pounding, as the officer scrutinizes it; It's standing in the middle of a cyclone in Malawi with your mother and promising her you'll get her home, even though you have no idea how.

It's not that I've never been afraid—it's that I've learned to move through fear. Vulnerability doesn't mean being unprepared; it means being open to the unknown. It means acknowledging that things will go wrong, that plans will fail, and that life will surprise you in ways you can't control. And it means knowing that even in those moments, you have the strength to keep going.

Every journey I've taken has been shaped by moments of vulnerability. Each time I've stepped into the unknown, I've found something greater than fear: resilience. And that's what I hope to share through this book—not just the destinations I've visited, but the moments that tested me, the people who supported me, and the lessons that shaped me.

Why I Travel

I don't travel to escape; I travel to understand. I travel to challenge the narratives we're told about the world and to replace fear with curiosity. I travel to remind myself—and others—that the world is far more welcoming than we often believe.

This book isn't a guidebook. It's a map of the lessons I've learned, the people I've met, and the moments that have changed me. It's a story of breaking down barriers and building connections.

It's a story of how my understanding of the world shifted. My travels—whether navigating checkpoints in Iraq, listening to the stories of Yazidis, or crossing borders with a pounding heart—gave me the kind of credibility no classroom or book ever could.

So, as you turn the pages, I hope you'll see not just the world through my eyes, but yourself in my story. I hope you'll find the courage to ask, "Why not?"—to step into the unknown, embrace your vulnerability, and discover the extraordinary strength within you.

Chapter I

INTO THE UNKNOWN I GO

For the strength of the Pack is the Wolf, and the strength of the Wolf is the Pack.

– From *The Jungle Book* by *Rudyard Kipling*

I've chosen to open with this quote from *The Jungle Book* because it's more than a childhood story for me. Growing up, I was enchanted by Kipling's tales of the jungle—how Mowgli coexisted with wolves, how every creature had its place. It wasn't just a story; it was a lesson about unity, survival, and the wild beauty of the unknown. It planted a seed in me, a deep-rooted fascination with wild places and the delicate dance of coexistence between humans and nature. Even now, 35 years on this planet, the echoes of those tales guide me as I travel to the world's most misunderstood corners.

But my journey didn't start in a jungle or on an African savannah; it started in the modest, warm kitchen of my maternal grandmother in Tamil Nadu, a woman who taught me the real meaning of community and hospitality. My grandmother was an artist, a creator who expressed herself through cooking, painting, and her deep care for everyone around her. She had an extraordinary talent—she'd watch a cooking show on TV, jot down notes, and recreate the dish with her own twist. She didn't bother following recipes; it was more about understanding the flavors, sourcing the finest ingredients, and bringing people together over shared meals. Every week, she would call in the entire neighborhood—often those who had the least—and feed them without question. It was a gesture of generosity that went beyond charity; it was her way of nurturing a community.

I carry her spirit with me in my travels, in the way I connect with people from all walks of life. It's why I'm drawn to places where hospitality isn't a transaction but a genuine act of kindness—a shared meal in Uganda, a cup of tea in Afghanistan, an unexpected gift from a stranger in Syria. These are not moments you find in the pages of a travel brochure, but they are the moments that stay with you long after the trip is over. They are the essence of what I seek when I explore: the simple, profound human connection that transcends borders and language.

From my experiences, one thing is clear: I was never meant to follow the conventional path. My family raised me with a strong sense of freedom and individuality. We weren't the type to chase after the *American Dream* of a green card, a mortgage, and a picket fence. At 25, my husband and I made the bold choice to leave behind the U.S. and the so-called stability it promised. We packed our bags with no safety net, no job offers waiting for us, and moved to Dubai. It wasn't an act of rebellion for rebellion's sake; it was a declaration of our values. We were determined not to let a lottery system decide our fate, not to become cogs in a machine that didn't serve us. We chose a different path—a path defined by risk, resilience, and the freedom to live on our own terms.

This decision was emblematic of the courage I carry into every journey I take. As a woman of color, I've had to challenge the stereotypes that society places on me, whether it's the expectation to settle down and start a family, or the narrow view of what an Indian woman 'should' be doing with her life. For us, family isn't defined by a child or a specific structure—it's defined by the love and partnership we share, even if it's just the two of us and our beloved pet. My grandmother taught me that nurturing doesn't require motherhood; it requires a generous heart and a willingness to break bread with anyone who comes to your table.

From Tourist to Storyteller

It was the pandemic that forced me to confront the direction my travels were taking. I had just returned from Antarctica in late 2019, and I was planning a trip to China when the world came to a halt. For someone who plans a year's worth of travel in January, the lockdown was disorienting. But it also gave me time—time to reflect on the places I had visited and the stories I had shared. I realized that while I had covered many iconic destinations, I had yet to dig deeper into the stories that mattered most to me.

I began to see my travels as more than a personal journey; they became a platform to challenge the narrative, to push back against the stereotypes I had grown up seeing in the news. I had always been fascinated by how the Western media portrayed certain countries, particularly those in the Global South—places like Syria, Burundi, or Afghanistan. They were often reduced to conflict zones, dangerous and chaotic, painted with a single, broad brushstroke. But I knew from my experiences that these places held immense beauty, resilience, and stories that went untold. So I made a conscious pivot. Instead of planning trips to popular, safe destinations, I started seeking out countries with complex histories and misunderstood reputations. It began with Burundi and Iran in 2022, and by 2023, I was venturing into the Congo, Syria, and Afghanistan.

Every time I traveled to these places, the first question I'd get was, "Is it safe?" The irony wasn't lost on me. I'd think about how someone could get shot while buying a gallon of milk in America, yet no one questioned the safety of that. The double standards were glaring, and it only strengthened my resolve to explore these countries and share their stories.

This journey isn't just about seeing the world; it's about redefining it. It's about challenging my own fears, pushing against the limits that society places on us, and asking myself constantly: *Why not?* I'm not interested in conforming, in doing what's expected of me as an Indian woman, a wife, or even as a traveler. I travel because it's the truest expression of my freedom, my curiosity, and my defiance. And I share these stories not to boast, but to break down the barriers of misunderstanding, to bring a little more truth into the world.

This book isn't a guide; it's a map of the places I've been, both literally and figuratively. It's a journey of pushing past the fear of the unknown, of finding my place in the world's wild, untamed corners, and inviting you to join me—not as a reader or a tourist, but as a fellow explorer. This is the tale of a wolf who wandered far from her pack, a lone adventurer roaming the uncharted wilds, armed with a little more than curiosity, grit, and a "weak passport" that could barely hold its own in the face of global red tape. In a world divided by borders, barbed wires, and bureaucratic stamps, my passport was never an all-access pass—it was a skeptical glance, a prolonged interrogation, a casual dismissal. Yet I carried it like a badge of pride, as a reminder that even the flimsiest piece of paper couldn't cage the urge to roam freely across borders.

For those of us from the Global South, every border check becomes a test of endurance, patience, and sometimes, the art of creative explanation. My "weak" passport, laughed at by international standards, now holds over a hundred stamps from places far off the usual traveler's map. It's seen me through deserts and jungles, through bustling city streets and quiet mountain paths. Over time, each visa stamp became less about collecting destinations and more about defying the odds. The thrill wasn't in crossing off bucket-list landmarks. Instead, my journeys were born of a desire to shake loose the restrictive stereotypes and cautious "no's" that society so easily hands women, especially women of color. I wanted to show myself—and the world—that fear has no place in our pursuit of wonder, and that borders, when you look closely, are just lines drawn by others.

I believe in a world without borders, a world that celebrates its colors and contrasts. I believe the question *Why not?* is one of the most powerful tools in anyone's life, a compass and a shield that guides us into places others call "off-limits." And I believe that every journey, whether to the remote towns of São Tomé or the familiar mountains of Uganda, is a step toward dismantling not just geographical boundaries, but the fears and beliefs that keep us from living fully.

In each new place, I encountered not only strange landscapes but also lives that pulsed with a richness I couldn't ignore—stories woven into the earth and sky, voices that spoke of endurance and beauty, quiet yet fierce, always at odds with the labels others had given them. I realized that fear is a brittle thing, something that thrives in ignorance and distance but shatters when we get close enough to see and feel the truth. With each step, I saw beyond what the world calls "dangerous" or "foreign," and found instead a familiarity—the warmth of home, the resilience of people, the shared laughter and struggles that make us all kin. Each encounter rewrote the story I'd been told, replacing what I'd "heard" with what I now knew, deeply and truly.

Travel, for me, has become an act of reframing—not just my own worldview but the narratives my culture clings to, the assumptions we carry without question. Every gesture of kindness, every laugh shared over language barriers, deepened my resolve to bring back a new vision—one that defies fear, erases stereotypes, and cherishes the humanity that binds us all. In Kabul's bustling markets, surrounded by the heady mix of spices and silk, strangers welcomed me with a curious warmth that felt like a distant kinship. Democratic republic of Congo introduced me to a silverback gorilla up close, revealing harmony with nature. São Tomé, with its unhurried rhythms and quiet charm, felt like a gentle whisper of how life can be when stripped down to nature's heartbeat. And on Hormuz Island in Iran, where ochre sands bled into turquoise waters, I found a kaleidoscope of colors that felt both surreal and fiercely real, like stepping into a world reborn.

In these places, so often overshadowed by misunderstanding, I learned that boundaries and fears are constructs—handed down from generations and rarely questioned. Standing in each of these spaces, I felt those boundaries dissolve, replaced by a profound sense of belonging that defied language, race, and history. The world, I discovered, is an open invitation, one that asks us only to step closer and look beyond the surface to find a shared humanity that transcends all.

Afghanistan Gave Me a New Pair of Eyes

Picture this: Kabul, Afghanistan. The market hums with life, a swirling mosaic of vibrant spices, glinting silks, and a warm chaos that only comes from a place deeply rooted in history. Vendors call out, their voices layered in laughter and negotiation, as children peek out from behind their mothers, their eyes full of naive inquiry.

I wasn't the outsider I had expected to be, nor the visitor they expected either. Instead, I was welcomed as a guest of honor, an unlikely stranger whose presence seemed to lift the spirits of those around me. The streets, which the world often paints with strokes of fear and danger, revealed instead a portrait of warmth, resilience, and hospitality, despite the burdens the people here had long carried.

It wasn't just the people who surprised me, but the landscape too. Afghanistan is a land of untold beauty. With each grain of sand bearing a survival story, the immense desert spreads out like an old tapestry. The towering mountains seem to watch over the land with an eternal calm, their snow-capped peaks framed against a sky so vast it feels like it could swallow the world. Here, the ground beneath my feet didn't feel like dirt—it thrummed with a quiet strength, as if the very land had learned to endure, just as its people had.

The world may rarely see Afghanistan's beauty, but I was fortunate enough to witness it, and I left knowing that this land is more than the headlines ever captured.

When I Went Into the Heart of Africa

In Uganda, the air smells of wet earth, alive with the deep fragrance of vast rainforests. The mist curls around the towering trees, weaving through the branches like a hushed secret. I stepped quietly into a world where time seemed to pause, only to be brought back to the present in the form of a silverback gorilla. His eyes held stories untold, a history that stretched far beyond my understanding. Standing there, I wasn't a visitor—I was a witness. A momentary participant in the vast, untamed story of the forest, where nature breathed and pulsed around me in ways that words could never capture. It was humbling, this reminder of how small we are, how fleeting we are, and how precious each moment truly is.

From the rainforest to the banks of the Congo River, my journey unfolded further into the heart of Africa. Here, life moved with a rhythm all its own—an unhurried beat that seemed to echo the timeless flow of the river. Along the riverbanks, the laughter of children filled the air, their voices carrying over the sound of the steady current. Women washed clothes in the water, their movements graceful, as if dancing to the rhythm of the earth. The Congo that I encountered was not the war-torn, fractured land often portrayed in the media, but a place of daily life guided by mundane activities of the day, where resilience was woven into the very fabric of existence. It was a place where joy and hardship existed side by side, where the human spirit, despite its struggles, managed to thrive. Here, I didn't just see a river—I saw the heart of Africa itself, pulsing with life, unbroken by the narratives imposed on it.

Raw and Wild in São Tomé and Príncipe

I stumbled upon São Tomé and Príncipe in a way that seemed almost serendipitous, a volcanic archipelago that felt like a lost world, tucked away in the heart of the Atlantic Ocean.

Isolated yet remarkably rich in character, this tiny paradise unfolded before me like a secret only the earth had been keeping for centuries. The jungle here is not just lush; it's a relentless cascade of greens, so vibrant that it feels as if the forest is alive, breathing in rhythm with the island's pulse. The air smells of damp earth and ripe fruit, a mixture of wildness and sweetness that dances with every breeze. The beaches are equally extraordinary, their pristine sands so white and untouched that they seem almost unreal, as if nature herself had sculpted them just for you.

Evenings on the island feel like stepping into a painter's dream, where the horizon is streaked with the softest shades of pinks and purples, and the ocean mirrors the sky in an unbroken line of serenity. The beauty is overwhelming in its simplicity—no high-rise hotels or bustling streets to obscure the view, just nature—unfiltered and unrestricted. In this tranquil corner of the world, time feels like it slows down, and with it comes a rare opportunity to listen deeply—to your thoughts, the whisper of the waves, the rustle of leaves—and to witness the vastness of the stars above, unmarred by the noise and light pollution of cities. It's a place that invites you to shed the busyness of life and to simply be.

São Tomé and Príncipe aren't places to rush through; they are lands that beg to be savored, their raw beauty unfolding slowly with each passing moment. The dense jungles are untamed, their shadows thick and cooling as you walk beneath a canopy alive with the hum of unseen creatures. With each step, you're led deeper into a world that feels both ancient and untouched, where nature's abundance exists without interruption or interference. There are no grand resorts or tourist crowds here, just an overwhelming sense of stillness, where you can lose yourself in the rhythm of the island—whether that's watching the clouds change shape over the mountains or feeling the coolness of the ocean as it laps gently against the shore.

This is the kind of place where the simplicity of life becomes its most profound feature. The days are unhurried, the people welcoming without pretence, the landscape untouched by commercialization. It's an opportunity to enter a world where people are treated more as kind visitors than as intruders, and it's an escape into nature at its purest. São Tomé and Príncipe is a reminder that beauty can often be found in places we least expect, in the quiet corners of the world that remain undisturbed, waiting for those who are willing to seek them out.

Discovering the Unexpected Colors of Iran

Iran is a land of paradoxes, where the colors of the earth and the spirit of the people collide in an unexpectedly beautiful tapestry. On Hormuz Island, the landscape is a surreal mosaic of color, where ochre-red cliffs stand in stark contrast to the deep cobalt blue of the surrounding sea. The golden sands stretch endlessly, meeting the horizon in a seamless embrace, while turquoise waters lap gently against the shore, creating a vibrant backdrop to the fiery landscape. This is an uncharted realm that defies the expectations of the outside world—a place where color and form exist in perfect harmony, free from the rigid definitions that often limit how we see the world.

But it's not just the landscape that leaves an impression—it's the people. Iran's warmth, hospitality, and openness are so often overshadowed by media portrayals, and yet, when you step into their world, you encounter something far more profound: a complex, layered humanity that challenges every preconceived notion. The conversations I shared with the people of Hormuz were a revelation, each story offering insight into a culture that is as vibrant as its surroundings. Their pride in their heritage and their resilience in the face of adversity painted a portrait of a nation that is far more than what we have been made to believe in for so long.

Iran is not a place that readily fits into the neat boxes we try to put it in. It's a country that revels in contradictions, and that is perhaps its greatest gift. The vivid landscape of Hormuz Island is a perfect example of this—its wild, colorful terrain is almost otherworldly. Here, the earth speaks in a language of vivid oranges, fiery reds, and electric blues, telling a story of resilience and natural wonder. The contrasts between the sand and the sea, the land and the sky, are so sharp that they feel like the work of a master artist—each brushstroke meant to highlight the raw, untamed beauty of this forgotten paradise.

Beyond the landscapes, Iran's true soul lies in its people. As I traveled deeper into the island's heart, I found that every encounter was an opportunity to peel back layers of misunderstanding. The people of Iran, often misrepresented in the global media, are some of the most hospitable and open-hearted individuals I have had the privilege of meeting. They were eager to share their history, their culture, and their lives, challenging the stereotypes that have long been attached to their homeland. Iran's true beauty lies not in the monuments or the landscapes alone, but in its people, whose kindness and resilience paint a much richer picture than the one often shown to the world.

About the Book

With every journey, I wanted to push past yet another invisible boundary, to challenge yet another notion of where women could or should travel, especially as women of color. I wanted to demonstrate that the world is far more welcoming than many believe. My experiences defied expectations at every turn; in these misunderstood lands, I found not only adventure but connection, compassion, and an abiding sense of shared humanity.

For a woman of color, traveling alone can be an act of rebellion, a refusal to let others define the limits of my world. In each country, I discovered strength in challenging not just the stereotypes around these places, but also the subtle limitations often placed on female travelers—expectations of safety, of propriety, of restraint. My journeys became a testament to the idea that women, especially women of color, can travel wherever curiosity calls them, breaking the bonds of fear and tradition with each step.

As I share these stories, I hope they serve as a call to anyone who has ever been told "no"—anyone who's ever been told a place, an experience, or even a life itself is out of reach. There is strength in embracing curiosity over caution, and there is freedom in challenging the boundaries that others set for us. This book is my journey beyond the surface, organized not just by place, but by the layers of discovery I unravel when I challenge stereotypes and dare to see the world through a different lens. It's divided into three sections, each capturing a unique essence of the lands I explore starting with misunderstood nations followed by the wildest countries and lastly by countries that have been least visited.

Misunderstood Nations

The first section reveals places that have been misrepresented or misunderstood—countries that defy the preconceived notions the world holds about them. These are lands painted by the media with broad, often inaccurate strokes—nations whose true character is often overshadowed by sensational headlines. Here, I venture past the narrative of fear, conflict, and hostility, uncovering the warmth, pride, and resilience of their people. These countries invite me to look closer, to see them not through the lens of media stereotypes but through the stories, faces, and experiences that are far richer and more complex.

Take Afghanistan, for example. Often defined solely by its struggles and conflicts, Afghanistan's true spirit lies in its vibrant cultural history and the resilience of its people. Kabul's bustling streets are alive with color, where artisans craft intricate rugs, and locals offer a hospitality that defies the portrayal of fear often seen in the media. In the Panjshir Valley, the land's rugged beauty and relentless spirit of its people speak to a history far older than war—one marked by ancient traditions and a deep sense of community. These places show me Afghanistan's true heart, a place of deep pride and culture.

Similarly, Syria is often reduced to images of destruction. But in cities like Palmyra, where ancient ruins still stand against the test of time, the country's historical and cultural significance becomes clear. Beyond the headlines, Syria's diverse landscape—from the Levantine coastline to the fertile plains—holds stories of ancient civilizations, inviting me to see beyond the destruction and witness the enduring beauty of its heritage.

Iraq, often overshadowed by its turbulent history, presents a complex and diverse landscape. In the Kurdish city of Erbil, ancient citadels overlook modern marketplaces, embodying a rich culture that remains steadfast despite recent challenges. The land, full of historical richness, from Babylon to Uruk, tells a story that transcends conflict—one of human achievement, pride, and survival.

The Wildest Countries

In the second section, I explore the raw, untamed beauty of nature's most powerful manifestations. These are the lands where the earth still feels untouched, and alive. From rugged landscapes to pristine beaches, towering mountains to dense jungles, these countries offer me a glimpse into nature's purest form. It's where the wildness of the world meets my deepest sense of awe, where human presence feels like a guest, and nature reigns in its most magnificent, unconstrained form. These places, still largely untouched by mass tourism, invite me to reconnect with something primordial—offering a chance to experience the planet as it once was.

Take Congo, for example the Congo River, cutting through the heart of the continent, is not just a waterway but a lifeline, nourishing the land and its people. The thick jungles and diverse wildlife here remind me of a world in its most primal state, offering an experience of nature's grandeur in its most raw form.

In Madagascar, the extraordinary biodiversity—ranging from bizarre baobab trees to unique species like the lemur—presents a land that feels like it's from another time. Madagascar's untouched landscapes, from the spiny forests to its pristine coastlines, preserve a world that's alien to most of us, offering glimpses of nature's most creative expressions, far from the influence of mass tourism.

São Tomé and Príncipe, a remote African archipelago, is another place where the raw beauty of nature remains intact. With its volcanic mountains, lush rainforests, and crystal-clear beaches, this hidden gem remains one of the world's least explored, offering a haven for me to experience nature in its purest form, far away from the distractions of modern life.

The Least Visited Lands

Finally, I travel to the world's hidden corners—places often overlooked by the average traveler, yet full of untold stories and cultural richness. These lands, the least visited, hold the kind of beauty that is often reserved for the few who venture off the beaten path. Here, history, culture, and everyday life blend together in a seamless dance, revealing a world that is both timeless and ever-evolving. In these countries, life unfolds at its own pace, untouched by the rush of modernity, preserving traditions and stories that might otherwise fade into obscurity. In these places, I am reminded that the world's most extraordinary experiences are often those that are the hardest to find.

Consider Sudan, a country rarely visited by tourists, yet rich with history. The ancient pyramids of Meroë, located in the Nubian Desert, rise silently from the sands, evoking a civilization that predates the famous Egyptian pyramids. Sudan's vast desert landscapes and untapped archaeological treasures stand in stark contrast to its portrayal in the media, showcasing a history that is still waiting to be explored.

Similarly, Turkmenistan, one of the world's most isolated countries, offers a glimpse into a land of surreal landscapes, like the Darvaza gas crater (the "Door to Hell") which burns with an otherworldly glow. The ancient ruins of Merv, once a thriving city of the Silk Road, offer an insight into a civilization lost to time, untouched by mass tourism. Here, in the isolation of Central Asia, I find a quiet beauty that few have the privilege to witness.

Gabon is another lesser-visited country where untamed wilderness reigns supreme. Its national parks, such as Loango, where elephants roam wild on pristine beaches, remain largely undisturbed by the outside world. Gabon's commitment to preserving its vast rainforests and diverse wildlife offers me a rare opportunity to experience nature in its most authentic and powerful form—far from the bustle of tourism.

Every chapter stands as a testament to the power of curiosity to conquer fear, of connection to dissolve boundaries, and of courage to redefine what's possible. And so, dear reader, I invite you to leave behind preconceptions, to embrace the question "Why not?" and to journey with me into a world that is waiting, open-hearted and far more welcoming than we have been led to believe.

Tips for Travelers

For those considering a journey through the countries mentioned in this book, it's essential to tread thoughtfully and with respect. Here are a few practical blanket tips:

- **Stay Informed**: Keep up with current travel advisories and stay in touch with locals for the latest information on safety.

- **Connect with Locals**: A local guide can be invaluable, not only for navigating the city but also for understanding its unspoken culture and traditions.
- **Respect Cultural Norms**: A simple greeting in Arabic or showing reverence at religious sites can go a long way in forging connections.
- **Be Flexible**: Plans can change quickly; allow space for spontaneity and be open to the unexpected.
- **Engage with the History**: Beyond the ruins, listen to the personal stories of the people—they add a depth to your experience that no museum display ever could.

MISUNDERSTOOD AND EXTRAORDINARY

The misunderstood often carry within them the sparks of the most extraordinary stories.

Tales from Afghanistan | Syria | Iraq | Hormuz Island Iran

Chapter II

AFGHANISTAN

September 2023

> ***We were scared, but our fear was not as strong as our courage.***
>
> ***– Malala Yousafzai***

There is a common misconception that travelers like me who venture into countries like Afghanistan are "crazy, fearless extremists." It's easy to imagine us as adrenaline junkies, people who thrive on flirting with danger, always in pursuit of the next wild experience to post about. In reality, nothing could be further from the truth. Trips like these are not impulsive decisions or reckless escapades. Instead, they are the result of months of meticulous planning, a slow build-up of courage and preparation—not just logistical, but mental and emotional too. By the time I physically step into a place like Afghanistan, I've already made the journey a hundred times in my mind, mapping out each scenario, every risk, every potential escape route.

There is a common thread that connects today's travelers—whether they're backpacking through Southeast Asia or taking a guided tour through Italy's vineyards—they crave the unknown, the authentic, the kind of experience that transforms more than just an Instagram feed. But there's a line between seeking adventure and courting real danger, a line that I tread carefully. My trips aren't fueled by a death wish; they're guided by a deep sense of curiosity and a desire to peel back the layers of a place that most only see from a distance, filtered through the lens of the evening news.

I do a thorough study of the country beforehand, asking myself a series of essential questions: Where are the danger zones? What areas are relatively safe? When is it absolutely off-limits to travel, and when might there be a relative lull in the turmoil, a brief window where I can slip through undetected? I pour over news articles, track the historical patterns of conflict, and sift through local forums, piecing together a jigsaw of insights from travelers who have gone before me. I'm not trying to tempt fate; I'm building a roadmap that could mean the difference between a seamless adventure and a disaster.

Before the Trip

Battling Resistance Within and Without

In May 2023, when I first entertained the thought of traveling to Afghanistan, it felt audacious even by my standards. It wasn't a simple whim or a fleeting curiosity—it was a deliberate choice that consumed my thoughts for months. I was knee-deep in research, sifting through guides, forums, and anything I could find that might help me understand the logistics, risks, and realities of traveling there. For me, finding the right guide is always the first and most important step. Without someone I could trust completely, I knew I wouldn't go.

After contacting several guides, I narrowed it down to two. Both were responsive, but one stood out—his replies were prompt, his pricing reasonable, and he seemed to understand the complexities of a solo female traveler navigating Taliban-ruled Afghanistan. Still, every email exchange revealed new limitations: places I wouldn't be allowed to visit as a woman, rules that seemed to change on a whim. Between my planning and my departure, several sites I had hoped to see were suddenly declared off-limits. It was a constant game of adjusting expectations.

By the time I brought it up with Anand, I was already halfway committed in my mind. I shared the idea casually while we were in Guyana, still riding the high of that adventure. His reaction was swift and predictable: "No, not now. We'll talk about it later." That "later" stretched into weeks, then months.

After returning home in June, I knew I had to face the conversation head-on. "I'm going," I told him one evening. "You can't be serious," he said, and I could see the frustration etched into his face. "Do you even understand what this means?" Of course I understood—or at least I thought I did. What I didn't expect was the internal battle that would rage within me for weeks after. Was I making a selfish choice?

Would my presence there inadvertently support a government I found abhorrent? Was I contributing, in some twisted way, to the silencing of Afghan women? These questions kept me up at night. I confided in my closest friends, people whose opinions I valued deeply. Some were supportive, others apprehensive. "This is huge, even for you," one said. "Are you sure you're ready for it?"

I wasn't entirely sure. But I was determined.

By July, I had made up my mind, despite my family's continued resistance. My husband tried everything to dissuade me—logic, guilt, even silence—but my resolve only strengthened. I wasn't looking for permission; I needed them to understand that this journey wasn't about defiance or recklessness. It was about growth, about pushing my limits as a traveler and as a person. The days leading up to my departure were fraught with anxiety. I pored over articles, guides, and firsthand accounts, trying to prepare myself for what lay ahead. I obsessively messaged my guide, asking about routes, checkpoints, and safety protocols. Every new piece of information brought a mix of excitement and dread. When the day finally came, I boarded the flight with a heavy heart. My family was still upset, Anand barely spoke to me, and I could feel the weight of their worry. But I knew there was no turning back.

The Journey

Afghanistan was everything I had anticipated and nothing I could have prepared for. Every step felt like walking a tightrope, balancing my curiosity against my vulnerability. On the fourth day of my trip, I found myself on a 15-hour drive to Bamiyan. As you will read later in this chapter, the journey was grueling—winding mountain roads, endless Taliban checkpoints, and a palpable sense of tension.

The two men accompanying me, strangers I had no choice but to trust, told the guards I was their sister and that we were heading to a hospital. I slept in the back seat, partly from exhaustion and partly to avoid drawing attention to myself. Even now, thinking about it makes my stomach churn. How did I sleep so soundly in a car with two strangers, under such precarious circumstances? There were moments when the fear was almost paralyzing. At one checkpoint, the guard's gaze lingered a little too long, his expression unreadable. I kept my head down, clutched my scarf tighter, and tried to disappear. The looks of contempt from the Taliban were a constant reminder of my place in their world—less than invisible, less than human.

Yet, amidst the fear, there were moments of profound beauty. The rugged landscapes of Bamiyan, the warmth of the families who welcomed me into their homes, the stories shared over cups of tea—all of it reminded me why I had come. These were real people, living under unimaginable circumstances, yet their hospitality and resilience shone through.

Yet, even in the shadow of dread, beauty persisted—raw and unyielding. The jagged cliffs of Bamiyan, carved by time and conflict; the defiant warmth of families who sheltered me in homes with crumbling walls; the laughter and lamentations traded over steaming cups of shir chai—these fragments anchored me to purpose. Here were lives reduced to survival, yet still ablaze with humanity.

One long night, when we had to drive overnight through the mountains to get to Bamiyan, I huddled with my guides in the car, lit only by flickering lanterns in the mountainside homes. Diesel fumes hung thick in the air as generators growled against the darkness. A former translator for the government, my guide now navigated a precarious existence, wondering if he can ever bring his family back from Pakistan. "We thought Kabul would never fall," he confessed, his knuckles whitening. "The Americans promised... Then one dawn, the city slipped from our hands." Through the smudged window, Taliban flags billowed like shrouds over ministry buildings - a ghostly presence where tricolor banners once flew.

In Bamiyan, I met a family of 5 living in a cave, the mother's face etched with decades of storms. She had endured the Soviet tanks, the Taliban's first reign, and the thunder of explosives that toppled her valley's ancient Buddhas. "Our bazaars once hummed with traders from Samarkand, Kashgar..." she murmured, her fingers tracing the frayed edge of her shawl. In her crumbling mud-brick home, she gestured to her son, hollow-eyed at the window. "Now he trembles at footsteps. The Taliban recruit boys who linger in the streets."

Every soul carried a variation of this fractured history. Painters who once splashed Kabul's walls with vibrant murals now hid their brushes. Ex-police commanders, once hunting the Taliban, became the hunted, drifting between safe houses. Shopkeepers bartered half-empty shelves; students buried textbooks; mothers rationed hope.

Still, generosity endured. Families with nothing pressed the last morsel of food onto my palm, refilled my cup with tea they could not spare, and smiled as if defiance could be brewed like chai. "We Afghans have mastered the art of survival," my guide remarked bitterly as we passed Darul Aman Palace, its skeleton blackened by rockets. "But survival is a corpse that still breathes. Our bones know how to persist. Our hearts...?" He trailed off, the silence louder than the wind.

The Aftermath

Returning home was bittersweet. Anand barely spoke to me for a week. His worry had turned to quiet anger, a mix of frustration and relief. Every update I had sent him during the trip was met with a terse acknowledgment. The 15-hour stretch when I had no network had nearly driven him and my family to despair.

In the days that followed, I found myself grappling with new questions. What had I accomplished? What did my presence there mean? I couldn't shake the images of women in full burkas, the hollow looks in their eyes, the stark reality of their lives. I felt helpless, frustrated, and deeply aware of my own privilege. But I also felt a sense of clarity. Traveling to Afghanistan wasn't about solving its problems or changing its realities. It was about bearing witness, about understanding the complexities of a place so often reduced to headlines. It was about acknowledging the humanity of the people I met, even if I couldn't change their circumstances.

This trip tested me in ways I never imagined—ethically, emotionally, and physically. It forced me to confront my fears, my privilege, and my purpose as a traveler. And though it left me with more questions than answers, I know it was a journey I was meant to take.

Back to the Trip

Now that you know that back story, I'd like to return back to the most important decision one has to make in choosing the right local guide. It's a process I take as seriously as choosing a co-pilot for a solo expedition. After months of scouring TripAdvisor's forgotten forums, cross-referencing whispers from many blogger groups, and cold-messaging Instagram accounts with single-digit followers, I have long learned to vet guides like a paranoid detective. Trusted contacts emerge only after relentless digging—checking multiple articles and blogs for references, grilling them on hyperlocal routes, and sensing their transparency when money is discussed. Even then, I'd ignore polished promises; the right guide often speaks in pragmatic half-sentences, knows when to lower their voice, and shares scars, not sales pitches. No spreadsheet replaces the gut-punch moment you video call them: Do their eyes stay steady? Does their advice feel *lived*? These guides aren't just facilitators who help translate a few words or find a shortcut—they are lifelines. They are the key that unlocks the doors to hidden alleys, unspoken stories, and the secrets of a place like Afghanistan. Without them, I'd be just another tourist on the surface, skimming the superficial layer of a country I don't truly know. On this trip, my guides were more than just companions—they were my safety net, risking life and limb for me, challenging the TBAN's authority on several occasions. They navigated the complexities of local politics with a deftness I could never hope to replicate, negotiating at checkpoints, coaxing and at times pleading, so I could see a new side of Afghanistan. In places like Afghanistan, your guide isn't just a fixer. Trust nothing, but especially yourself.

As a tourist in Afghanistan, you are part of a larger spectacle, an unspoken performance where you play a small but significant role. You are unlikely to face overt harassment—it's part of the regime's calculated effort to present a facade of "openness and friendliness." This isn't just a hospitality gesture; it's a strategic manoeuvre to craft a narrative that might attract foreign interest and, eventually, investment. Is it a facade? Most likely. Beneath the polite smiles and hesitant welcomes, you can sense the tension, like a low hum beneath the surface. Just know that TBAN checkpoints are scattered like sentinels, standing guard every few miles, each one a reminder of the unseen forces shaping your journey. If you think you can traverse Afghanistan without bumping into them, you're mistaken. They are a part of the landscape now, as ingrained as the jagged mountains that outline the horizon.

For me, each city came with its own ritual—a formal introduction to the TBAN head, a kind of gatekeeper who had to be placated before I could explore further. Every encounter started the same way, a mix of cautious glances and stilted pleasantries as they tried to find "the right words in Pashto" to address me. It felt like stepping into a strange dance, their words careful, almost rehearsed, as if they were reciting lines from a script they hadn't fully mastered. And always, there was a look of surprise that flickered across their faces, as if asking: "What are you doing here? Are you alone? How did you think of coming by yourself? Haven't you read the news?" I've come to expect these questions, delivered with a blend of shock and curiosity. I meet them with a steady gaze, a small smile that reveals nothing. "Hindustani? Mashallah!" they exclaim, as if my nationality alone is enough explanation for my presence.

Their questions are not just idle curiosity—they were testing me, gauging my reaction, perhaps hoping to see a flicker of fear. But I knew better than to give them that satisfaction. My husband's words echoed in my mind, "Pick your battles, stay quiet, and get out. Keep things in perspective. Don't get emotional." It's a mantra I repeat to myself in moments of doubt, a reminder to maintain my calm, to keep my face neutral and my intentions hidden.

Meeting women here is like trying to capture a shadow—they're elusive, often out of reach. In the markets, I found a few, but they were scared to share, their voices tinged with fear. It's a difficult realization to know that as an outsider, my presence offers no real shield, no protection for them. I am a temporary visitor in a world where the stakes are much higher for them than they are for me. They are cautious, guarded, and I respect that. I don't push; I nod, exchange a glance that carries unspoken understanding, and move on.

I'm not here to paint a romanticized picture or to downplay the reality. The media isn't always wrong—this time, some of it is true. The men with guns, the surveillance, the constant checkpoints—they are all very real. But what the media often fails to show is the other side of life here. Yes, there are armed men patrolling the streets, but there are also children playing soccer in dusty alleyways, shopkeepers arguing over the price of melons, and families gathering for tea as the sun sets behind the mountains. It's almost 'safe' to visit now, by Afghan standards, if you come with the right permits and a local guide who knows the ropes.

Still, I'll be honest with you, Afghanistan isn't for everyone. It's not a place you come to on a whim, with a casual shrug of the shoulders. It requires unlearning, a willingness to strip away everything you think you know, to confront your own biases and fears. I didn't need to be brave to come here, but I did need to place an enormous amount of faith—in strangers, yes, but also in myself. It's a kind of trust that only travel can teach you, an unspoken contract between you and the unknown, a leap of faith that you take again and again.

Traveling to Afghanistan pushed me to my limits, as the best kind of travel always does. It peeled back layers of my own insecurities, forced me to confront my deepest fears, and showed me sides of myself I hadn't met before. This is a country that moves to the rhythm of its own heartbeat, a land steeped in the prayers that echo off its ancient, jagged peaks. Until you're there, shoulder-to-shoulder with the people who call it home, you can't possibly understand its full story. The injustices, particularly toward women, are undeniable.

But to reduce Afghanistan to just that would be a disservice to its complexity. There is another side here, a side I am trying to show you—a side that, if you're willing to look closely enough, might just surprise you.

Shir-Khan Bandar Border Crossing

The Unplanned Test of Will

The Shir-Khan Bandar border crossing was one of those moments in life that seem ordinary on paper but etch themselves into your memory with an intensity you can't shake off. I had left Dushanbe, Tajikistan, with a naive sense of triumph, convinced I had planned everything down to the last detail. After hours of being crammed into a shared taxi, sticky with the sweat of strangers and the dust of the road, I finally arrived at the border—only to find my confidence shattered within seconds.

The immigration officer barely glanced at my papers before his eyes flicked up to meet mine. His expression was a mix of incredulity and disdain as if my very presence were an affront. "Woman," he said slowly, the word dripping with derision. "Alone." It wasn't a question; it was a verdict. Solo female travelers weren't just a curiosity here—they were an anomaly, a scandal even. At that moment, I felt every ounce of my preparation evaporate. I was no longer the well-researched traveler armed with guides and permits; I was simply a woman, alone, in a place that didn't know what to make of me.

For four long hours, I stood there, helpless. The border crossing, a mundane act for most, had transformed into an excruciating trial of endurance. Time slowed, stretching into an unbearable silence punctuated only by the sound of my own racing heart. I could feel the doubts clawing at the edges of my resolve. Had I made a mistake? Was this a line I shouldn't have crossed? But then, as if fate decided to intervene, an elderly Afghan man appeared. He didn't say much—just a few quiet words to the officer and a slight nod in my direction. He paid my fee without hesitation, taking me under his wing with a simple gesture that spoke volumes.

The relief I felt wasn't just about getting through the border; it was about the unexpected kindness, the humanity that cuts through layers of fear and politics. He guided me toward a family traveling in the same direction. Their smiles, warm and genuine, were a stark contrast to the hostility I had just faced. We waited together, and as we chatted, the mother, to my delight, spoke Hindi. She shared my story with her family; her voice was tinged with a sense of pride. It struck me then – this was the Afghanistan you don't hear about—a place where strangers become friends and people show up for you without expecting anything in return.

Mazar-i-Sharif

Beauty and Broken Promises

Mazar-e-Sharif, the "City of Peace," is a name that drips with irony. In the heart of this storied city stands the Blue Mosque, a radiant masterpiece of Islamic architecture. Its shimmering tiles, an ocean of turquoise and sapphire, catch the morning light and glint like fragments of the sky itself, casting an ethereal glow across the plaza. But beneath the mosque's stunning facade lies a deeper dissonance. Only two weeks before I arrived, a new rule had barred women from entering this sacred space—a decree that rendered the idea of peace almost hollow.

Standing outside, I felt a pang of exclusion. The mosque was a monument to serenity, yet the barred doors felt like a symbol of the ongoing erasure of women's rights in this turbulent land. I watched as men went in, the rhythmic call to prayer wrapping around them like a warm blanket, while I stood on the fringes, an outsider in more ways than one. The city, with its vibrant bazaars and the hum of daily life, seemed to carry on as if nothing had changed. But for me, the denial of entry felt like a fissure opening up—a reminder that this journey would not be an easy romance with a mystical land. Afghanistan was testing me, forcing me to confront both its splendor and its scars. It wasn't a place to be loved lightly; it demanded patience, and a willingness to hold opposing truths in the same breath.

As I wandered away from the Blue Mosque, the sun began its descent, casting long shadows across the bustling streets. I knew then that Afghanistan wasn't here to indulge my traveler's fantasy—it was here to unravel it. Yet beneath the surface of my frustration, a flicker of hope still danced. Perhaps, somewhere beyond the contradictions, lay a trace of the tranquility that this city was once known for.

Samangan

The Silence of History

Samangan was like a mirage, appearing unexpectedly on my journey with a sense of ancient wisdom. The landscape was rugged and unforgiving, yet it cradled a serenity that belied the turmoil of modern Afghanistan. Here, nestled in the rocky folds of the mountains, stood Takht-e-Rustam—a Buddhist stupa carved into the earth itself, dating back to the 4th century. It felt like a defiant whisper of history, untouched by the chaos that had swept across the country for centuries.

As I began my climb up the mountain path, I could feel the layers of history thickening around me. Each step seemed to carry me further back in time, past the modern conflict, beyond the reach of the Taliban, and into a forgotten era where Buddhism flourished in this very soil. The air was thin at the summit, and my breaths came in shallow gasps, but the sight below was worth every labored inhale. There, gleaming in the afternoon sun, lay the stupa—solid, silent, and eternal.

I stood, transfixed by the sheer resilience of this monument. It was as though the land itself had decided to hold onto a piece of its past, a time when Afghanistan was a nexus of trade, culture, and spiritual exploration. The silence was profound, almost reverent, as if the mountain held its breath in respect for the ancient structure. I sat down at the edge of the cliff, my legs dangling over the side, feeling a wave of awe wash over me. It wasn't just the view—it was the palpable sense of continuity, of something too powerful and sacred for even the harshest forces of destruction to erase.

At that moment, I realized that Afghanistan's beauty wasn't just in its landscapes but in the tenacity of its spirit. This stupa was a quiet act of resistance, a testament to the idea that history could survive in the cracks of a broken present. I took a deep breath, letting the stillness sink into my bones, knowing this feeling—this awe—would follow me for the rest of my journey.

Panjshir Valley

A Testament to Resilience

The car rattled and groaned beneath me, each bump on the road sending jolts up my spine as if the journey itself were testing my resolve. We had left Samangan hours ago, the sun long gone, replaced by the bone-chilling darkness of the Afghan night. Fifteen hours had passed in this metal cage, hurtling through jagged mountain passes and skirting the edges of valleys still bearing the scars of war. The sound of the engine, grating and relentless, was our only companion, punctuated by the jarring pauses at checkpoints. The flash of a flashlight, a glint of metal in the moonlight—each stop was a reminder of where we were, a land where every few miles, someone held a weapon and a question.

At around 3 a.m., as my eyes fluttered between exhaustion and a strange kind of trance, my guide turned to me, his voice a raspy whisper cutting through the engine's roar. "Panjshir," he said, as though the name itself held magic. And perhaps it did, because despite the fatigue weighing on me, a thrill shot through my veins. I had dreamed of this place for months—a hidden valley, a sanctuary of resilience.

The darkness began to lift as we rolled into the Panjshir Valley, the first light of dawn painting the jagged peaks of the Hindu Kush in soft hues of pink and gold. It was like emerging from a tunnel into a world untouched by time. The valley stretched before us, a green ribbon of life cradled by the mountains. Villages clung to the slopes, tiny dots of color against the vast, rugged landscape. The air was crisp and cool, carrying the scent of pine and the faint melody of a stream rushing somewhere nearby.

My guide pointed toward a group of children playing by the water's edge, their laughter ringing out, pure and joyful, like a song carried on the wind. They wore clothes that had seen better days—faded, patched up, but meticulously cared for. Their faces, small and sunburnt, were marked with the kind of resilience that belies their age. They had been born into a land that had seen more conflict than peace, yet here they were, blissfully unaware of the burdens their elders carried. It felt like a moment suspended in time, a glimpse into the unbreakable spirit of Panjshir. I stood there, taking it all in—the laughter, the play, the simple joy in the midst of a place known for its history of resistance. The Panjshir Valley was more than just a geographical marvel; it was the heart of

Afghanistan's fight for freedom, a symbol of defiance etched into its very rocks. For decades, the people of this valley had fought off invaders, refusing to bow down to any force that tried to break their spirit. Even today, with the shadow of the Taliban looming, Panjshir stood tall, unyielding, its people like the mountains that cradled them—scarred but steadfast.

I watched the children until the sun climbed higher, their laughter fading into the distance as we moved deeper into the valley. I realized then that this place was a paradox—both a haven of peace and a battlefield of resistance. And it was this duality that made it one of the most profound places I had ever visited. It was a place that demanded to be felt, not just seen.

Bamiyan

The Sorrow of Lost Heritage

Bamiyan felt like stepping into another realm, a place where the land held stories far older than any living memory. This picturesque valley, nestled in the arms of the Hindu Kush, was once the westernmost frontier of Buddhist expansion. The colossal Buddhas that had once stood here, carved into the sandstone cliffs, were now only empty niches—a stark reminder of what had been lost to time and conflict. Yet, despite their absence, the spirit of the place lingered, woven into the very fabric of the soaring cliffs that surrounded the town.

I decided to hike up to Shahr-e-Zohak, the "Red City," named for its rust-colored cliffs that blazed in the setting sun. As I made my way up the steep, winding path, I felt as though I were ascending into history itself. The cliffs were pockmarked with caves and tunnels, an ancient labyrinth that had once been homes, temples, and places of meditation. The cool darkness of the caves was a welcome respite from the sun, but emerging into the light again brought a wave of awe that washed over me like a tide.

At the top, I was greeted by a group of mountain villagers. Their faces, tanned and weathered, told stories of hardship and endurance. They lived on the edge of existence, surviving on a mere pittance, yet they welcomed me as if I were family. A family of five led me into their cave dwelling. It was a space carved out of the cliffside, where they shared a simple meal of flatbread and tea. We sat together on the cold stone floor, the silence between us filled with an unspoken understanding. There, in the dim light, I felt the weight of their kindness—a warmth that transcended the barriers of language, culture, and circumstance.

A young girl, no older than seven, caught my eye. She sat quietly in a patch of sunlight, playing with a smooth, rounded stone, her small fingers tracing its surface as if it were a precious gem. On impulse, I knelt beside her and asked, "Do you go to school?" The light in her eyes flickered momentarily, a shadow crossing her innocent face. Her mother stepped forward, her expression one of resigned sorrow. "Girls," she said softly, almost apologetically, "...they are not allowed to learn." The words hung in the air like a weight I couldn't shrug off. Here, amidst the remnants of a civilization that had once embraced knowledge and spiritual growth, a young girl's future was being stifled by the very soil that had birthed so much enlightenment. My throat tightened, a knot of helpless rage and deep sadness forming. I wanted to scream at the injustice, but the mother, sensing my turmoil, simply patted my hand. Her touch was gentle, a gesture of comfort that spoke volumes.

As I left the family's cave and descended the path back toward the town, the sun dipped below the horizon, casting long shadows across the valley. The Buddhas were gone, their absence a gaping wound in the cliffs. But I wondered if the greater loss was not in the statues themselves, but in what they represented—a culture of learning, of open-mindedness, now obscured by a veil of ignorance. I turned back for one last look at the cliffs before they disappeared into the darkness. The question lingered in my mind: Does hope still live here? Despite everything, a small part of me wanted to believe it did. For if hope could endure in a place like Bamiyan, then perhaps it could endure anywhere.

Band-e-Amir Lakes

Marveling through Tension

The journey to Band-e-Amir wasn't without its fair share of drama. This shimmering chain of turquoise lakes, cradled by the rugged cliffs of the Hindu Kush, had been on my bucket list for years. I had pictured myself standing on the edge, marveling at the crystalline waters that seemed to mirror the boundless Afghan sky. But as we approached the park entrance, reality struck. Women were no longer allowed to visit these sacred lakes—not even tourists like me, with permits in hand. My guide, Hassan, a man whose kindness and fierce loyalty had come to embody the legendary Afghan hospitality, squared his shoulders and refused to back down. A flicker of defiance sparked in his eyes as he launched into a heated argument with the Taliban officers.

I couldn't understand the rapid flow of Dari, but the gestures and the tension in the air were unmistakable. Hassan was gesturing toward me, toward the paperwork, his voice rising and falling like the crash of waves against a cliff. He was fighting for a sliver of freedom, for a chance to show this foreign woman the beauty of his homeland, a place she had journeyed so far to see. The minutes dragged on, each one stretching into what felt like an eternity. My anger simmered beneath the surface, but I knew that raising my voice would only make things worse. Instead, I stood there, calm and resolute, offering silent support as my guide argued on my behalf.

Then, something shifted. The lead officer, a man with a stern face and eyes hardened by years of war, gave a curt nod. There was a flurry of paperwork, and then, miraculously, Hassan turned to me, grinning from ear to ear. He handed me a small slip of paper—a special permit, a hard-won victory. Relief washed over me, mingled with a deep gratitude for this man who had gone to battle for me with nothing more than words and a stubborn sense of what was right.

The lakes unfolded before me like a painting brought to life, each one a different shade of blue, shimmering in the light of the morning sun. It was a breathtaking sight, the kind that no camera could truly capture. I felt a pang of guilt, a shadow across my joy. I was here, standing at the edge of this natural wonder, soaking in its raw beauty. But for the local women, this solace was denied—a simple pleasure taken away, a reminder of the harsh, invisible chains they carried. It felt like a hollow victory. As a woman traveling in Afghanistan, I had learned to take things as they came, to choose my battles wisely. How does a feminist reconcile with this kind of contempt? By remembering that it isn't about me, by knowing when to walk away, even when it stings. I stood there, looking out over the pristine waters, and realized that my visit was a small act of defiance and a quiet insistence that beauty and solace can still be found, even in a place marred by injustice. The lakes reflected the sky, unbroken and pure, as if offering a glimpse of a world where freedom isn't a privilege, but a right. I hoped that one day, the women of this land might stand here too, free to share in this moment of peace.

Kabul

Stepping Back in Time

The first light of dawn spilled over the ancient city of Kabul, casting a golden glow on its dusty streets. I wandered through the quiet morning markets, immersing myself in a sea of vibrant colors and heady scents. Pomegranates, ripe and ruby red, spilled out of wicker baskets; the smell of fresh bread wafted through the air, mingling with the earthy aroma of saffron and spices. Despite everything—despite the conflict, the uncertainty—Kabul's soul was still very much alive, pulsing with a rhythm of resilience and hope that no regime could quash. No trip to this bustling capital would be complete without seeking out the legendary Haji Miraman. Down a narrow alleyway, in a tiny, dimly lit studio, he sits—the last kamra-e-faoree *(instant camera)* photographer in Afghanistan. The box camera, an age-old relic from a bygone era, sits proudly at his side. It's a work of art in itself, a wooden contraption that requires expert handling and just the right kind of photo paper. Haji Miraman has spent a lifetime mastering this craft, shooting portraits of people outside his home, where the sun serves as his lighting, casting a soft, natural glow that no studio setup could replicate.

Watching him work was like stepping back in time. His hands moved with the kind of ease that comes from decades of practice, adjusting the lens, positioning the camera, coaxing his subjects into just the right pose. He spoke with a quiet pride about his art, about how this camera had survived the Soviet invasion, the civil wars, the first rise and fall of the Taliban. It wasn't just a camera—it was a witness to history, capturing fleeting moments in a city that had seen more change in a century than most do in a millennium. He invited me to sit for a portrait, and as I did, his young grandson hovered nearby, watching intently. It struck me then—the continuity, the passing of skills and stories from one generation to the next, even in a place where so much has been lost. The click of the camera was followed by a flurry of activity, a delicate dance of developing the photo right there on the spot. When he handed me the finished portrait, I couldn't help but smile. It wasn't just a photograph—it was a piece of Kabul's heart, a little slice of its spirit that I could carry with me.

The morning sun climbed higher, bathing the city in light as I bid farewell to Haji Miraman and his family. I walked away with the photo clutched in my hand, a priceless souvenir and a reminder of the quiet, everyday moments that make this city so extraordinary. Kabul is a place where hope persists, not in grand gestures or sweeping changes, but in the simple, resilient act of living—of creating, of sharing stories, of passing down a craft that refuses to die, even in the face of adversity.

The People

Sharing a steaming cup of chai with a rug seller in Kabul, I listened to his story. His weathered face, lined by years under a harsh sun, softened as he spoke of his family. He shared memories of loss—his brother was taken by a stray bullet years ago. Yet, there was no bitterness in his voice, only a quiet acceptance. This was the famed Afghan spirit: enduring unimaginable hardships while still clinging to hope.

I saw that same hope shining in the eyes of a young girl I met in a sprawling UN refugee camp near Mazar-e-Sharif. Clutching a worn notebook, her face lit up with determination, a striking contrast to the flimsy tent that was her home. Her resolve was unshakable, which was an inspiring testament to the strength of the Afghan spirit.

On another scorching afternoon, as I wandered through the maze of Herat's old city, an elderly man tapped my shoulder. Despite our language barrier, his concern was evident. He gestured toward a nearby tea stall and insisted I sit down to cool off with a glass of chilled *doogh*, a refreshing yogurt drink. It was impossible to refuse his hospitality. As I sipped the drink, the stress of the day slowly melted away, replaced by a deep appreciation for this simple kindness.

However, I was acutely aware of the privileges I enjoyed as a foreign tourist. I was granted courtesies and protection that many Afghan women are denied. In just eight days, I was only scratching the surface of life here, but I was determined to share an honest perspective of my experience. The hospitality I encountered was overwhelming, reminiscent of the warmth I had felt in Japan. Yet, my heart ached every day. Sometimes it was with joy, touched by the kindness of strangers. Other times, it was a sharp, painful ache when confronted with the remnants of war or the stories of terror. The contrast in Afghanistan is stark—one moment, I was sharing hot chai in the Bamiyan mountains, the next, I was arguing with the TBAN, or covering myself with a full burqa. Despite everything, there is life here, vibrant and unyielding.

Dispelling the Myths

Let's be honest, Afghanistan isn't on many people's travel bucket lists. But sometimes, the journeys we least expect become the most transformative. Stepping off the plane, a wave of relief swept over me—not because I had arrived safely, but because I felt a stereotype shatter in that moment. The fear I had carried while planning this trip began to dissolve the moment I met my guide, who greeted me with a warm smile. This was the start of a new story.

Contrary to the prevailing image of a country steeped in hatred and tension, I found pockets of peace amidst the struggle. Security concerns were real, but they didn't overshadow everything. Laughter filled the air in shops, families strolled through parks, and children chased pigeons in squares. Life, though undeniably marked by suffering, carried on with a quiet resilience.

Before I arrived, I was haunted by the image of women hidden beneath burqas, stripped of agency. In reality, I did see women wearing burqas, and I respected their choice. But I also met women with just a headscarf, out shopping or dining in restaurants. I encountered artists displaying their work and students eager to pursue their education. The media portrayal isn't entirely inaccurate, but it's not the whole story.

War documentaries paint Afghanistan as a desolate land, but I found a country of breathtaking beauty. The Band-e-Amir National Park, with its turquoise lakes framed by rugged mountains, looked like a scene from a dream. The fertile valleys of Bamiyan, dotted with the remains of ancient Buddhas, whispered tales of a grand history. Even the chaotic streets of Kabul, lined with century-old mosques and bustling tea houses, held a charm that was impossible to resist.

Was it Worth It?

The first question I get is always the same, *"Afghanistan? Alone?"* The surprise is understandable. My answer is simple: It's a land of astonishing beauty, rich history, and people whose warmth left an indelible mark on me.

Were there challenges? Absolutely. In conservative areas, the burqa felt less like a garment and more like a shield, offering a sense of safety. There were moments of intense loneliness, the sting of missing a shared experience. Yet, there were also moments of profound connection. I drank endless cups of chai with locals who peeked curiously from behind colorful headscarves, eager to learn about my faraway home. I listened to their hopes and dreams, often for a world that overlooks them.

"Weren't you scared?" people often ask. I'd be lying if I said there weren't moments of fear. I checked security updates more frequently than usual. But fear can be a cage. Instead, I focused on being prepared—hiring a reputable guide, researching local customs, and dressing modestly. The Afghans responded with kindness and an openness that surprised me. The people in my hotel couldn't have made me feel more at home, and families repeatedly invited me into their homes, offering meals and heartfelt conversations.

"What was the food like?" is another common question. Afghan cuisine is a delight. Fluffy naan dipped in minty yogurt sauce, spicy *Aushak* dumplings, and sun-dried apricots—all remnants of the ancient Silk Road—were just a few of the highlights. But the food was only part of the experience. Sharing a meal in Afghanistan is an act of deep connection, a way of forging bonds over plates of some of the best meals I've ever had.

"Did you see the war-torn areas?" Yes, the scars of conflict are everywhere. Bullet-riddled buildings stand as silent witnesses to a troubled past. But alongside this devastation, there's a spirit of rebuilding. Children attend makeshift schools, and there's a palpable sense of pride in their heritage, as there should be. Every day brought moments that left me humbled.

Would I recommend it? Afghanistan isn't for everyone. It demands respect for traditions, a willingness to adapt to unexpected challenges, and an adventurous spirit. But for those who dare to step outside their comfort zone, Afghanistan offers an experience unlike any other. It will challenge your perceptions, open your eyes to a way of life far removed from your own, and leave you with a sense of connection that transcends borders and cultures.

Chapter III

SYRIA

February 2024

> ***The most dangerous thing a woman can do is go searching for herself—and find her own wild, untamed spirit waiting on the other side.***
>
> ***– Clarissa Pinkola Estés***

When I first spoke aloud the words *"I'm going to Syria,"* the reaction was immediate, a collective inhale that seemed to draw all the air out of the room. The atmosphere grew taut, charged with a disbelief so palpable I could almost taste it. *"But why Syria?"* The question wasn't so curious as it was laced with a thinly veiled alarm. My friends and family stared back at me with expressions that teetered between bafflement and outright panic, as if I had just declared my intent to walk straight into the mouth of a dragon.

To them, Syria was a country trapped in a perpetual state of collapse—a montage of bombed-out buildings, desperate refugees, and a sky thick with smoke. It was a place synonymous with war and ruin, a stark, cautionary tale replayed on the news until it became little more than background noise. They couldn't understand why I would willingly venture into a land marked by conflict and why I would choose to see what so many turn away from.

For me, Syria was never just a casualty of war. It was a place where the echoes of ancient civilizations still lingered in the streets, where the scent of cardamom and jasmine mingled in the evening air like an old love song. Syria was a hymn, a story sung in a language the world had forgotten how to listen to. I felt its pull like a distant, haunting melody, as if the land itself was calling me to witness what lay beneath the scars. I wanted to feel the heartbeat of this place, raw and steady, like the pulse of blood beneath a bruised surface.

This was not a decision made lightly; it was a kind of rebellion, a refusal to be ruled by the fear that had already claimed so many minds. I was driven by something deeper, a yearning to touch the raw, unpolished edges of the world, to reach for the stories buried beneath rubble and ash. I needed to look beyond the headlines, to see the faces and hear the voices that defied the narrative of a broken nation. I needed to breathe the same air that carried both the whispers of old prayers and the smoke of burning rubble.

This wasn't just about travel; it was about seeking something the maps couldn't show me, something that existed in the spaces where history and humanity intersected. I was searching for the wild, untamed spirit of a place that refused to be defined by its wounds. I wanted to witness the resilience that blooms like wildflowers through the cracks in a shattered sidewalk, fragile yet fierce in its persistence.

In choosing Syria, I chose to follow the unknown, to let it lead me into places where hope and despair danced together in a strange, tragic rhythm. It was an invitation to sit with discomfort, to confront my own fears and prejudices. I knew there was a risk in this—of course I knew. But the greater risk, I realized, was in staying away, in never hearing the stories that could only be told by those who had lived through the darkness and still found a way to embrace the light.

For every ruined building, there were people rebuilding. For every scar, there was a memory of a time before the wound. And I wanted to see it all, to collect these fragments of human spirit, like pieces of colored glass washed up on the shore after a storm. I was a woman on a quest—not for answers, but for the questions that only a place like Syria could ask, the kind of questions that shift something inside you and rearrange the very fabric of your soul. And in that search, I knew I would find a part of myself I had never met before, waiting patiently on the other side of fear, wild and untamed, ready to walk beside me into the unknown.

The Waiting Game

Before Syria

Syria wasn't supposed to be this hard. But then again, nothing about traveling to one of the world's most volatile regions ever is.

I returned from Afghanistan in September 2023, still riding the emotional rollercoaster of that journey. Eight days there had left me exhausted yet exhilarated, unsure whether I was more in awe of the experience or the fact that I had survived it. But even as I unpacked my bag, I was mentally packing for the next destination: Syria.

Everything was planned meticulously, as always. Months of preparation had gone into it. Security clearance? Check. Flights? Booked. Guide? Confirmed. By October, I was ready to board a flight to Lebanon and begin the crossing into Syria. It was all set—until it wasn't.

War broke out. The news came fast and chaotic, as it often does in the Middle East. One moment, it was a simmering tension; the next, it was an explosion of conflict. My phone buzzed relentlessly as I scrambled to message my guide. "What now?" I hoped for answers that wouldn't come.

"Wait and watch," he said. "This region works like that—if it happens in one place, it spills everywhere."

It was maddening, the not-knowing. I couldn't even call it uncertainty; it was a certainty that things were falling apart. Each day, I obsessively refreshed the news, my heart sinking with every update. October came and went in a blur of escalating violence and frantic back-and-forth messages. My guide was patient but firm: "If you want to cancel, I understand. If you want to wait, we'll make it happen."

So I waited. November wasn't any better. By then, I'd already pushed the trip once. My security clearance—a painstakingly obtained document that took a month to process—had expired. The clock reset, and I had to start again. Each time I applied, each time I waited for that elusive green light, it felt like the universe was daring me to give up.

But I didn't. December rolled around, and I thought, *This is it. It's happening.* My guide was cautious but supportive. "The call is yours," he told me. And so, I called it. I pushed the trip again.

By January, I was in a state of limbo so intense that even the smallest decisions felt monumental. Should I pack? Should I wait? Should I give up entirely? Every day felt like living in the shadow of a decision that refused to be made. And yet, amidst the chaos, I clung to a gut feeling.

"If I don't go now, I'll never go," I finally told my guide.

This time, he didn't hesitate. "Let's do it."

I reapplied for security clearance for the third time, rebooked my tickets for the fifth, and prepared myself for what I knew would be an ordeal. The journey to Syria wasn't just about the physical crossing—it was about navigating an emotional minefield of doubts, fears, and the relentless "what-ifs" that plagued me every step of the way.

By the time I landed in Lebanon, the tension was palpable. The war wasn't just across the border; it was in the air, seeping into every interaction, every glance, every decision. The crossing into Syria was nerve-wracking, marked by endless security checks and a constant undercurrent of fear.

In Lebanon, the anxiety was almost louder than the conflict itself—a relentless whisper that something terrible was just around the corner.

But I crossed anyway. Looking back, the "before" of Syria wasn't just a prelude; it was a battle in itself. It tested my resolve, my patience, and my ability to push forward when everything seemed determined to hold me back. It wasn't easy. It wasn't supposed to be. But it was necessary.

And so, I went.

Maaloula

The Language of the Ancients

The streets of Maaloula wrapped around me like the folds of an ancient scroll, winding and narrow, leading me deeper into a story that felt older than time itself. I stepped carefully along cobblestones smoothed by centuries of footsteps, past stone houses with crumbling facades that seemed to lean in close, whispering their secrets to anyone willing to listen. The scent of wild thyme and rosemary hung in the air, carried by a breeze that rustled the ivy clinging to the walls. It was as if I had walked through a veil and emerged into another era, a place where the past had not yet learned to loosen its grip.

A woman's voice, clear and gentle, pulled me out of my reverie. "Do you know Aramaic?" she asked curiously in her soft voice. She stood in the doorway of a small shop, her fingers deftly weaving vibrant threads into intricate patterns. The fabric seemed to dance in her hands, alive with color and history. I smiled, shaking my head. "I'm just a traveler who wants to learn," I said, the admission feeling both humble and honest in this ancient village.

She laughed, a sound like water cascading over stones—light and melodic. "You're not alone," she said, her eyes crinkling at the corners with a kind of quiet amusement. "Many come here, searching for a piece of the past. Our history runs deep, like roots in the rocky soil." She pointed up toward the cliffs that loomed above us, where ancient monasteries clung precariously to the rock face, as if held there by sheer will. "This place has seen so much. And yet, we are still here."

There was a fire in her gaze, a defiant spark that seemed to challenge the world's perception of this place. I felt a kinship with her, a shared understanding of what it means to exist in defiance of expectation. "What drives you?" I asked, genuinely curious about the source of her strength.

"The spirit of my ancestors...," she replied without hesitation. Her voice softened, but her eyes remained steady, full of a quiet, unyielding resolve. "...and hope."

I nodded, absorbing her words as I continued my climb higher into Maaloula. The village felt like a living prayer, with each alley and stone wall steeped in a reverence that was almost tangible. Here, history was not just a distant echo; it resonated in the very fabric of the place, in the whispered prayers and the songs carried by the wind.

The Monastery of St. Serge

Where Silence Speaks

The Monastery of St. Serge rose before me, stark and solemn, its stone walls weathered by time and conflict but standing tall, as if anchored by something far deeper than the earth it rested upon. The air inside was cool and still, filled with the faint scent of beeswax candles burning in silence. Their soft glow cast flickering shadows on frescoes that adorned the walls, depicting scenes of devotion that had witnessed centuries pass by.

An elderly monk approached, his steps slow but purposeful. He moved with a grace that suggested a lifetime of quiet contemplation. "Welcome," he murmured, his voice gentle, like the rustle of leaves in a breeze. He motioned for me to sit beside him on a worn wooden bench, its surface polished smooth by countless visitors who had come seeking solace.

"Thank you," I managed to say, though the words felt inadequate for the sense of peace that washed over me in that moment. It was as if the weight I hadn't realized I was carrying had been lifted, if only for a while.

The monk studied me, his eyes kind and infinitely wise, as if he could see the questions swirling inside my head. "What brings you to our land?" he asked, his tone inviting honesty.

"I want to understand...," I said, feeling a sudden rush of vulnerability. "...to see beyond what the world portrays." I thought of the images I'd seen in news reports—the devastation, the conflict, the pain. But here, in this quiet place, there was something the cameras had missed. Something that words could barely grasp.

He nodded slowly, as though he had heard similar sentiments countless times before. “Many come with fear in their hearts,” he said.

I took a deep breath, recalling the worry etched on the faces of those who had tried to dissuade me from coming here. “I have known fear,” I admitted, the memory of frantic news feeds flashing through my mind. “But there is so much more than violence.”

A small, knowing smile tugged at his lips. “Exactly,” he said with a gentle certainty that felt like a balm. “We live our lives in the midst of it all—love and laughter are part of it too, along with the pain.”

As if on cue, a burst of laughter echoed from outside, where children played near a stone fountain, their voices rising like birdsong. It was a sound so pure, so filled with life, that it cut through the stillness of the monastery and settled something deep within me. I glanced back at the monk, who was watching me with a quiet smile.

“Life finds a way,” I whispered, echoing his earlier words, feeling them settle into the core of my being like a truth I had always known but needed to be reminded of.

“Yes,” he replied softly. “That is what you take home.”

We sat together in silence for a moment longer, the only sound the faint crackle of candle flames dancing in their holders.

It felt as though time itself had paused, granting us this shared space to simply *be*—two souls connected by the universal language of seeking, of witnessing.

As I left the monastery, the sun was beginning its descent, casting a golden light over the village of Maaloula. The shadows stretched long, but the day was not done; there was still a warmth in the air, a lingering promise that this place, like its people, would endure. And as I walked away, the monk's words followed me, ringing like a bell in the stillness of my heart: *"That is what you take home."*

Krak des Chevaliers

The Fortress of Memory

The sun was barely a sliver above the horizon when I set off for Krak des Chevaliers. The early morning light bathed the landscape in a soft, golden hue, and the road ahead curved through rolling hills that seemed to stretch endlessly, like the folds of a giant green quilt. With each bend, a new vista unfolded—olive groves dotted with wildflowers, mist rising gently from the earth, and the occasional silhouette of a shepherd guiding his flock across the fields. It was peaceful, deceptively so, as if nature itself was whispering a quiet reassurance before the reveal of what lay ahead.

Nothing, not the photographs I'd seen nor the countless pages I'd read, could have prepared me for the first sight of it. Emerging from the fog like a phantom of history was the mighty Krak des Chevaliers, its stone walls towering above the landscape, austere and majestic. It stood there, a silent guardian of centuries, as if holding its breath and waiting for me to draw closer. My heart pounded, not from fear, but from the sheer awe of being in the presence of such a legend.

We parked the car and stepped out into the crisp morning air. The scent of damp earth and pine needles filled my lungs, grounding me in this moment of wonder. I stared up at the silhouette of the fortress, dark against the pale sky, like the spine of some ancient beast curled protectively over its hoard of secrets. This was the 'Castle of Knights,' a fortress that had withstood the ravages of time and war, standing as a testament to resilience and human ingenuity.

The entrance arch loomed before me—tall, imposing, yet carved with a grace that hinted at the craftsmanship of another age. As I stepped inside, I was met by Omar, my guide for the day. He was an older man, his face lined with the tracks of countless smiles and a life well-lived. His eyes, though, were what caught me—bright, alert, with a sparkle that made him seem as much a part of the castle as the ancient stones around us.

"Welcome," he said, his voice warm like the morning sun. He gestured for me to follow, and with a wave of his hand, invited me to step back in time. "Let's walk through history together."

Inside, the fortress felt strangely alive. Light streamed through arrow slits, casting slender beams that danced across the walls, illuminating carvings worn smooth by the hands of time. The air was cool, carrying the faint scent of moss and aged stone. As we climbed the spiral staircases—narrow, steep, each step uneven from centuries of use—I felt a connection to those who had walked here before me. It was as if their footsteps echoed beneath mine: the clanking of armor, the murmur of hushed voices plotting strategy, the laughter of soldiers seeking a moment of respite between battles.

When we emerged at the top, the world opened up beneath us in a breathtaking panorama. Valleys rolled out as far as the eye could see, a patchwork of green fields, ochre soil, and the silver shimmer of distant rivers winding their way through the land. It was easy to see why the Crusaders had chosen this spot—perched here, they must have felt invincible, as if the entire world lay at their feet.

Omar stood beside me, his gaze sweeping over the landscape like a man greeting an old friend. "This was once the heart of crusader defense," he said, his voice carrying a note of reverence. "From up here, they believed they could hold back any enemy."

I listened, letting his words sink in, but my thoughts drifted to the castle's more recent past. I knew that during Syria's conflict, Krak des Chevaliers had become a pawn in a new kind of war. The stones that had once shielded knights now sheltered fighters of a different era, and the fortress, for all its age, found itself woven into the modern narrative of a country in turmoil.

Omar's voice dropped, quieter now, almost somber. He pointed to a distant corner of the fortress, its stone darkened by smoke and time. "Over there," he said, "during the occupation, a local guard was taken hostage. He was the last to leave, held here for months."

I turned to him, the weight of those words settling like a stone in my chest. "How did he survive?" I asked, trying to grasp the fear and uncertainty that must have filled those days. Omar gave a small, reflective smile, "History is complicated," he said with a shrug. "But this place endures. Just like our people."

We continued our walk through the fortress, passing through vast chambers that had once echoed with the sounds of feasting knights and the clash of swords. Now, the silence felt sacred, a reverent hush that held the stories of a thousand years.

As we neared the end of our tour, I couldn't help but ask, "Do many people still come here?" I had expected the answer to be tinged with sadness, a lament for the dwindling numbers of those brave enough to visit a place so tied to images of conflict. But Omar's eyes lit up, his face breaking into a genuine smile. "Yes, they do. Every year," he said with a note of pride in his voice. "They come to see what remains of our heritage"

I hesitated, the next question forming slowly on my lips. "Aren't they afraid? Isn't it dangerous?" He looked at me thoughtfully, his gaze searching my face as if to measure the depth of my understanding. "Maybe they are, but fear is no excuse to stop seeking understanding. Those who come here are like you," he added, nodding slightly.

His words settled into the silence between us, carrying a weight I knew I would carry home with me. This journey wasn't just about seeing a monument; it was about bearing witness to a legacy of endurance, of a people who have weathered the storms of history and still stand, unbowed.

As we left the fortress, the sun hung low in the sky, casting long, golden shadows across the ancient stones. It was a moment suspended in time, where past and present seemed to meet in the glow of the fading light. I took a deep breath, filling my lungs with the scent of the countryside one last time. The Krak des Chevaliers had shown me something far more powerful than its imposing walls—it had shown me the strength of a spirit that cannot be broken, the heartbeat of a land that, despite everything, still pulses with life.

And as we drove away, the silhouette of the fortress receding in the rearview mirror, I felt that I had not just visited a place, but had become part of its story.

Homs & Aleppo

A Tale of Ruins and Resilience

The sun hung low in the sky, casting a golden, melancholic light as I made my way into Homs. The rugged hills I had driven through gave way to the sprawling cityscape, a chaotic symphony of defiance and decay. The road narrowed, and the atmosphere thickened, as if the very air carried the weight of memories steeped in blood and ash.

Homs had been the stage for some of the most harrowing violence in Syria's recent history. The echoes of conflict seemed to hang around me, not just in the charred buildings that lined the streets, but in the very bones of the city. There was a strange, haunting beauty in its brokenness. I parked near the city center and stepped out. The streets were a tapestry of contrasts. Some buildings stood tall, their facades marred by bullet holes but still defiantly upright, like soldiers who refused to bow. Others had crumbled into heaps of rubble, dreams shattered alongside the stone, leaving behind gaping windows that stared out like hollow eyes—witnesses to the tragedies they had housed. Yet, as I walked further into the city, I was struck by the life that still thrummed beneath the surface, like a heartbeat you only notice when you're very still. The marketplace buzzed with activity, vibrant despite its bleak surroundings. Vendors called out, their voices a lively melody that filled the void left by the silence of abandoned homes. I paused at a stall where a woman was selling pomegranates. The fruit's bright red skin seemed almost audacious against the gray backdrop of the ruined city.

"Fruit!" she called in her clear and strong voice, filled with a resolve that made me pause. I approached her stall, compelled by her energy.

"How do you keep going?" I asked, unable to hide the awe in my voice. Her smile faltered for just a heartbeat before she steadied it, like a sail catching wind.

"Life must go on," she replied simply, her words a quiet declaration of survival.

The Road to Aleppo

By the time night had fallen, I found myself back at the hotel in Homs, the fatigue of the day heavy in my limbs. But my mind was alight, buzzing with the scenes I had witnessed—the juxtaposition of ruin and resilience, the fragility and strength of a place determined to endure. I lay awake for hours, replaying the images in my head: the marketplace, the defiant woman with her pomegranates, the crumbling buildings that seemed to tell their own silent stories.

The next morning, anticipation sparked within me like an electric current as I joined the drive to Aleppo. The road stretched ahead, a ribbon winding through a landscape marked by the scars of war. As we neared the city, the streets grew narrower, hemmed in by walls pockmarked with bullet holes and mortar blasts. The buildings seemed to lean inwards, as if they had grown weary of standing tall, their once-proud facades now drooping under the weight of too many memories.

The moment I stepped into Aleppo's Old Town, I could feel its heartbeat—a quiet, persistent thrum beneath the rubble. The Citadel loomed above me, a stone guardian that had watched over its people for centuries. Its ancient walls, scarred but unyielding, seemed to carry the weight of both sorrow and hope, as if they held stories buried deep beneath layers of dust and time.

I walked slowly through the winding, crumbling streets, taking in the sights and sounds of a city still struggling to find its rhythm. The silence was thick, punctuated only by the occasional creak of shifting debris or the distant murmur of voices. It was here, amidst the ruins, that I came across three boys, their small hands clasped together as they navigated the rubble. None of them could have been older than ten, their laughter bright and pure, cutting through the somber stillness like a knife.

I watched them for a moment, mesmerized by the simple joy they radiated in a place where joy seemed impossible. They noticed me, their eyes wide with curiosity, and stopped in their tracks.

"What are you doing here?" asked the boldest of the three, his voice clear and direct.

"I'm here to learn about your city," I said, smiling at them. They exchanged glances, as if weighing the truth of my words.

"We're exploring!" chimed in another boy, bouncing on his toes with excitement.

"Do you live here?" I asked gently. The first boy nodded, his small face serious for a moment as he gestured to a deserted building nearby. The walls of the building were crumbling, and the paint faded to a dull, lifeless gray.

"This was our playground before," he said quietly, the ghost of a smile tugging at his lips.

"Is it fun anymore?" I ventured, not sure if I wanted to hear the answer.

They looked at each other, a shared, unspoken understanding passing between them before one of them spoke up with a sheepish grin. "We make it fun," he said simply. Their voices, so light and matter-of-fact, soared with a kind of innocence that seemed almost magical in the face of their surroundings.

Without warning, one of the boys called out, "Want to see something cool?" He was already racing ahead, his small form darting through an alleyway strewn with trash and shards of shattered glass that glinted in the sunlight like pieces of broken dreams. I followed them as they wriggled over the remains of a low wall. When we rounded the corner, I stopped short, my breath catching in my throat. Before us was a hidden garden, a tiny oasis amidst the destruction. Wildflowers had taken root in the torn earth, their vibrant petals reaching upward toward the sunlight that filtered through the broken beams above. It was a beautiful, unexpected burst of life, a vivid splash of color against the gray of the ruins.

"It's beautiful!" I exclaimed, turning to look at the boys. They beamed back at me, their pride shining brighter than any flower in that little garden.

"This is our secret place," one of them whispered, as if afraid the magic might disappear if the world knew of it. Their laughter rang out, filling the air, and for a moment, it felt like music—a sweet, pure melody that softened the sharp edges of the city's sorrow.

In that moment, standing there with these boys amidst the rubble, I felt a swell of hope unlike anything I had experienced before. It was a reminder that life finds a way, even in the harshest of places. These children, with their boundless energy and unbroken spirits, were proof that joy could take root anywhere, even among ruins. They were the flowers fighting their way up toward the light.

Palmyra

Echoes of Eternity

The next leg of my journey took me to Palmyra, a name that conjured up images of a mythic sorceress—an enchantress who held sway over desert sands and distant skies. It felt as though I was being drawn into the past, to a place where the crossroads of ancient civilization once thrummed with the vibrant exchange of spices, silks, and stories. Here, the remnants of a bygone era awaited me, whispering of grandeur and glory that once flourished in this desert oasis.

As I approached Palmyra, the air seemed to thicken with a palpable sense of unease. The road was dotted with checkpoints, stark concrete barriers jutting out against the serene backdrop of endless dunes. Armed soldiers stood watch, their eyes sharp and unblinking, a stark reminder of the fragile peace that held this land together. The contrast between the vast, quiet desert and the tense, watchful men was striking. It felt like driving through a mirage, where tranquility could dissolve into conflict at any moment.

At the first checkpoint, a soldier stepped forward and motioned for me to roll down my window, his eyes scanning my vehicle with the wariness of someone who had seen too much.

"Where are you headed?" he asked, his voice hard, like stone.

"Palmyra," I replied, trying to keep my tone steady even as my heart fluttered with a mixture of excitement and anxiety. He glanced at my passport, flipping through its pages with the practiced indifference of someone who had done this a thousand times. I could sense a flicker of uncertainty in his gaze, a question left unasked.

"Be careful there," he warned, handing back my documents with a slow, deliberate nod.

"I understand," I said, offering a small, reassuring smile. "But I need to see it for myself." He waved me through, and I drove on, feeling a shiver of unease settle in my bones. The road ahead seemed like a gauntlet, each checkpoint a test of endurance, with soldiers whose faces told silent stories of exhaustion and the burden of constant vigilance. It was as if the land itself was holding its breath, caught in a delicate balance between memory and reality.

Finally, the ruins of Palmyra came into view, and I felt a rush of awe wash over me. Columns of limestone rose against the sky like the fingers of a giant, stretching upwards as if trying to catch the fleeting sunlight. They stood tall and proud, remnants of an ancient world, their surfaces adorned with intricate carvings that spoke of long-lost gods and the glory of empires past. Yet, as I walked among these pillars, I couldn't ignore the signs of recent conflict—the scars left by bullets and shrapnel, the crumbling edges where once-perfect stones had been shattered by blasts.

I found myself standing before the Temple of Bel, its majestic facade partially collapsed but still exuding a dignified grace. It was impossible not to think of the footage I had seen in documentaries, of tourists wandering these grounds freely, marveling at the ancient architecture without a hint of fear. Now, the place felt eerily quiet, the silence thick and heavy.

As I moved through the temple's remains, I noticed a man standing by one of the columns, his fingers tracing the carved stone with a reverence that caught my attention. He was part of a local team of architects and archaeologists, painstakingly working to restore what they could of Palmyra's glory.

"These stones have seen empires rise and fall," he said without turning around, his voice soft yet filled with a kind of unshakable certainty. "They will outlast all of this." I stepped closer, watching the way his hands moved across the ancient carvings, almost as if he were reading the lines of a sacred text. "Are there many still working on the restoration?" I asked.

He sighed, the sound full of weariness. "Fewer than before," he admitted. "There are many restrictions now, and not everyone is willing to take the risk. But we do what we can. This is our history," he said, gesturing around us with a sweep of his hand. "We worry it will fade away, like sand blown off into the desert."

The sorrow in his eyes was unmistakable, a deep, aching grief for a legacy that might crumble to dust if left unattended. My heart clenched at his words. I realized that if one turned away too quickly, they might miss these stories forever.

As I continued to wander through Palmyra, the sense of security measures looming over me was more profound here than anywhere else I had been in Syria. The presence of armed guards and the sight of military vehicles patrolling the area were constant reminders that this place, once a beacon of cultural exchange and artistic achievement, now stood at the mercy of those who wielded power. It was an uneasy dance between safeguarding the ruins and stifling the spirit of a city that had once thrived on openness and movement.

Yet, amidst the ruins, there was an undeniable allure—a pull that went beyond the ancient stones and bullet-scarred walls. It was the feeling of standing at the edge of eternity, of connecting with something that had survived countless cycles of rise and fall, something that was both incredibly fragile and astonishingly eternal. I could feel it in the air, in the way the sunlight slanted through the broken arches, casting shadows that danced across the ground like fleeting memories.

I paused by a small, makeshift memorial, flowers placed at the base of a crumbling column. It was a simple tribute, yet it held a depth of meaning that seemed to transcend time. The flowers, delicate and vibrant, stood as a reminder that even here, life found a way to endure. In that moment, I felt a deep sense of gratitude for having the chance to witness this place, to stand among the ruins and feel the heartbeat of an ancient world.

As I left the ruins behind and made my way back to the road, I glanced one last time at the silhouette of the temple against the fading light. The columns stood tall, like sentinels guarding the stories of those who had come before. I knew then that this place, with all its scars and shadows, would stay with me forever—a part of the eternal dance between memory and time, a whisper of a tale that refused to be forgotten.

Damascus

My final stop on this week-long odyssey through Syria was Damascus—the city whose very name thrummed like a heartbeat, echoing the pulse of civilization's past. This ancient city, among the oldest continually inhabited places on earth, felt like the soul of Syria itself, stitched together with countless stories and lifetimes.

As I drove into Damascus, the skyline unfolded, a mosaic of domes, minarets, and stone buildings soaked in the warm hues of dusk. Parking on a narrow side street, I stepped out to the aromatic embrace of the city—spices, grilled meat, and the heady scent of jasmine. The streets pulsed with life: vendors called out, touting their goods, children zipped through crowds, and the chatter of the locals blended with the hum of passing cars. I lost myself in the winding alleyways of Old Damascus, a labyrinth where every twist and turn seemed to breathe history. The sun slanted down, illuminating the cobbled streets and casting long shadows that whispered of secrets. I arrived at the Umayyad Mosque, a sprawling masterpiece that seemed to shimmer under the last light of the day. The mosque's golden dome caught the sun's rays, gleaming like a beacon. I stepped into the vast courtyard, where tranquility reigned. The marble floor, cool beneath my bare feet, stretched out in a white expanse broken only by the ancient mosaics that adorned the walls—depicting paradisiacal gardens and rivers of turquoise.

The call to prayer began, and the sound rippled through the courtyard, a serene harmony that enveloped the space. Worshippers gathered in quiet clusters, heads bowed, the murmur of prayer a gentle counterpoint to the city's bustle beyond the mosque's walls. I stood at the edge, watching this ancient ritual unfold, a timeless moment that felt like stepping into the pages of a history book. Later, I wandered into the Souq al-Hamidiyeh, the heartbeat of Damascus. Under its arched, covered walkway, the souq (market) was a sensory feast—lanterns hung overhead, casting soft light on the vendors below, their stalls overflowing with vibrant fabrics, intricate jewelry, and jars of sweet, sticky dates. The smell of freshly ground coffee mingled with the sharp, earthy aroma of za'atar.

"Falafel?" A young woman called out, her smile wide and inviting. I approached her stall, where she deftly wrapped a piece of falafel in warm pita, adding crisp lettuce and a generous drizzle of tahini. One bite, and the crunch of the falafel gave way to a tender, herby interior. I nodded in delight. "Delicious," I managed to say between bites.

Her laughter was infectious. "The best in Damascus," she said proudly, handing me a small cup of mint tea. I took it gratefully, the sweet, hot liquid a balm against the evening chill setting in.

As night fell, I found myself seated in a small café beneath the canopy of the souq's stone arches. The tables were crowded with locals, families sharing platters of fruit and nuts, friends leaning close in animated conversation. I sipped on my mint tea, the steam curling into the air, and watched the scene unfold around me. It was easy to forget the checkpoints, the armed soldiers, the remnants of a war-torn past. Here, the laughter was full-bodied, the smiles genuine, and the spirit indomitable.

On my last day, I met an elderly artisan at his shop tucked away in a quiet corner of the souq. He was busy at work, carving delicate patterns into a piece of olive wood. I paused to admire his craftsmanship, the way his hands moved with such practiced grace. “This craft has been passed down in my family for generations,” he told me, glancing up with a smile. “It’s a part of our history, our way of remembering who we are.”

His words stayed with me as I made my way back to my car. The journey through Damascus had felt like peeling back layers of time, revealing the resilience and warmth of its people, the pride they held for their heritage. Yes, the scars of conflict were there, etched into the very stones of the city, but they did not overshadow the vibrancy of life that flourished in spite of them.

Driving out of the city, the golden dome of the Umayyad Mosque receded into the distance. I thought back to the laughter in the souq, the taste of the falafel, the solemn beauty of the mosque at sunset. Damascus, with its ancient spirit and undying heartbeat, had left a mark on me far deeper than any guidebook could have described.

Syria... *A Poem of Survival*

In Syria, I found myself surrounded by ruins, but not the kind made of stone. There were invisible fractures too—echoes of stories carried by the wind, borne on the voices of a people who refused to be silenced. Wandering through these streets, I was enveloped by a resilience that felt almost sacred. Here, the past and present intermingled like smoke and sunlight, and I realized that my own struggles were merely whispers in comparison to the roar of their survival.

I met an old man and his son in Aleppo, their home a skeleton of what it once was, cradled by the shadow of war. They had fled when ISIS stormed their neighborhood, leaving everything behind. Yet, when the battles quieted, they returned—not because the danger had passed, but because this place was their anchor. "This is our home," they said, as if there had never been another choice. It struck me deeply: this quiet, unyielding courage that clung to the land, the rubble, the memories. They weren't just rebuilding walls; they were piecing together fragments of identity, of everything that war had tried to steal from them.

I've known loss too—the kind that leaves you gasping, untethered. When my grandmother passed away, it felt like a rift opened up in my world. She was my north star, the one who raised me, the one whose hands held entire histories in their softness. Her death carved a hollow ache in me, a grief so profound it made me question everything I had once believed. And yet, even as I stood in the wreckage of my own sorrow, I knew that my pain paled in comparison to what

I witnessed in Syria. The people here had lost entire worlds, yet they carried on, heads high, with a grace that felt almost otherworldly.

If there's one thing Syria taught me, it's the power of surrender—not a defeatist giving up, but a release of the need to control what we never truly owned. There's a strength in letting go, in standing naked before the chaos and choosing to live anyway. It's Darwin's survival of the fittest, but it's not about physical strength. It's the kind of fitness that comes from bending without breaking, from finding a flicker of light in the darkest night.

In Damascus, I sat with shopkeepers who had lost everything but still offered me tea, smiling as if the world hadn't crumbled around them. My guide and his friends shared stories of better days, of childhoods spent in vibrant neighborhoods now turned to dust. And even as they spoke of loss, they would ask me about India. "Your culture is as ancient as ours," they said with a spark of pride. We swapped tales of history, of old songs and spices, and for a moment, it felt like time stood still, bridging the gap between what was and what could be.

I remembered a story my cousin told me long ago, when she visited Palmyra before the war. Her guide had reassured her then, "What's happening in Iraq could never happen here." Yet, when I stood in that same place years later, the unimaginable had become reality. It was a stark reminder of the fragility of our worlds, how quickly the unthinkable can unfold.

But the greatest lesson I took with me was this: we must never take anything for granted—our safety, our loved ones, the quiet, ordinary moments that make up a life. Every day is an invitation to rebuild, to find something worth holding on to, even when everything else feels lost. In Syria, I saw the strength to start over, again and again. It's a gift I carry with me, a reminder that no matter how deep the wound, there is always a way forward, always a reason to keep believing in the dawn after the darkest night.

Chapter IV

IRAQ

March 2024

> ***Survivors are the strongest people I know. We are not victims; we are witnesses to strength.***
>
> ***– Nadia Murad***

Iraq. The very name evokes a swirl of conflicting images: the birthplace of civilization, yet synonymous with relentless conflict. This is the land where the Tigris and Euphrates rivers nurtured the ancient cities of Ur and Babylon, where the stories of Gilgamesh were first etched into clay. Here, Mesopotamia birthed culture, law, and literature, long before modern borders carved up its rich tapestry. Yet today, these ancient wonders are obscured by the haze of war and political strife. I found myself yearning to see beyond that veil.

Our trip was not one of casual tourism. My husband and I came as seekers, intent on peeling back the layers of misconception that have hardened like sediment over the true heart of Iraq.

I wanted to trace the pulse of its present, to meet the people whose resilience defies the headlines. Beneath the rubble and ruin, I sensed an untold vibrancy—a nation that continues to live, laugh, and love despite the scars it bears.

As I shared my travel plans with friends and family, the responses were predictable: a mix of shock, disbelief, and genuine concern. "Why would you go there?" they asked, as if I had chosen to walk into a storm unprepared. Their reactions only fueled my resolve. For years, I had listened to one-sided narratives that painted Iraq in shades of grey—ruins, militias, destruction. But I envisioned something different: the vibrancy of Baghdad's bazaars, the scent of spices wafting through the air, and the sound of laughter weaving through stories shared over cups of strong, sweet tea.

In preparation, I immersed myself in maps and memoirs, ancient texts, and contemporary articles. Each source revealed another facet of Iraq's identity, a mosaic of cultures and histories: the Kurdish mountains in the north, the Arab heartlands at its center, and the traces of ancient Assyrian cities scattered like relics of a forgotten time. I wanted to connect with the voices that persisted here—voices of hope, of memory, of a future still in the making.

Our journey would take us from Mosul's devastated yet strong old city, where reconstruction efforts fight to reclaim its soul, to the storied Citadel of Erbil, one of the world's oldest continuously inhabited sites. We planned to listen and learn, to gather the fragments of stories often overlooked in Western media coverage. This was not a sightseeing expedition; it was a pilgrimage of understanding, a chance to witness a nation rebuilding itself piece by piece, memory by memory.

As we boarded the flight, the significance of our trip settled in—a weighty mixture of anticipation and purpose.

The descent into Baghdad was surreal. As the plane broke through the clouds, I caught my first glimpse of the city—the minarets piercing the sky, the Tigris winding its way through the heart of ancient Mesopotamia. It was sunset, and the golden light cast long shadows over the city's rooftops. I felt a rush of excitement, mingled with the solemn awareness of where we were about to land. This was the Baghdad of legends, the once-great jewel of the Islamic Golden Age, now bruised but still glinting with the remnants of its former glory.

As we were descending, my husband quickly pointed out the window. "Look at that," he said, gesturing toward a neighborhood where children played football in the fading light.

"It's beautiful," I replied, surprised by how normal it all seemed—children laughing, the call to prayer echoing through the streets, families gathering for their evening meals.

This was the Iraq I had come to find: not a battlefield, but a living, breathing country. A place where life continues despite the weight of its history, where ordinary people go about their lives with a quiet, unyielding strength. It was here, in these moments of everyday normalcy, that I began to see the true essence of Iraq.

The trip had a clear mission: to capture this untold beauty, to challenge the narratives of despair, and to share the stories of a nation that, despite everything, still sings its own song. As the plane touched down, I knew that what lay ahead would change not only my view of Iraq but also my understanding of the world. This journey was about more than just travel; it was about bearing witness, about seeing the unseen, and about allowing Iraq to tell its story in its own voice.

A Tale of Yin, Yang, and Babylonian Blues

Introducing Anand into the narrative feels like opening a secret door to an entirely different layer of adventure—a quieter, more cautious one, but no less fascinating. While I'm the firebrand who leaps into the unknown, Anand is the water that tempers my flames, keeping our adventures from turning into outright chaos. He's the yin to my yang, or as I like to say, the brakes to my runaway train.

He's not just my husband; he's my balance, my brakes, and one of the most fiercely feminist men I've been lucky enough to have in my life. While I'm all about chasing the story, throwing caution to the wind, and venturing into places most would consider a hard pass, Anand is the steadying force that keeps me grounded—or at least tries to.

This trip to Iraq was quintessentially me. I mean, I live for these experiences—the untold stories, the behind-the-scenes realities, the history etched into every brick of a ruin. That's my heartbeat. Anand, on the other hand, is the history buff who loves his textbooks, documentaries, and carefully curated museum exhibits. But here's the thing: he's risk-averse. Extremely risk-averse. He works for an American company, which means Afghanistan, Syria, and Iran are not just off his bucket list; they're off the map entirely.

"No way," he said the first time I brought up Iraq. "This is not happening."

But I'm persistent. From December, I started my campaign—strategic nudges, earnest pleadings, the occasional, "Come on, this is a once-in-a-lifetime opportunity!" He countered with logic and safety statistics. I countered with my usual mix of enthusiasm and charm.

By March, after four months of relentless nudging and the persuasive power of, "You'll regret it if you don't," he finally relented. By the time we boarded the flight, he had done enough risk analysis to rival a CIA operative. Me? I was already dreaming about the ruins of Babylon and the stories of the Yazidis I hoped to learn firsthand. Anand's initial discomfort was palpable the moment we landed. While I buzzed with excitement, he scanned the airport like a hawk, eyes darting between exit signs and security personnel. Every checkpoint, every bag scan—it was all a fresh reminder of the volatile region we were in.

And while Anand may not have shared my sense of adventure, he respected it. That's what makes him so remarkable.

As much as he may have protested initially, his feminism shines in the way he supports my passions, even when they clash with his comfort zone. But something fascinating happens when you throw two opposites into an extraordinary setting. We started to see Iraq not just through our own eyes but through each other's. For Anand, Iraq was a lesson in stepping out of his bubble and the awe of walking through the ancient Babylon Gardens, the realization that he was standing in the cradle of civilization itself. For me, it was about the stories—the Yazidi families rebuilding their lives, the remnants of Mosul's devastation, and the silent resilience of people living amidst ruins.

I'll never forget the dinner at our guide's home. He shared stories of how ISIS tried to breach Kurdistan's borders, of alarms going off in the dead of night, of families forced to flee with nothing but their lives. Anand listened intently, I could see his usual calm exterior betraying a flicker of unease. It was a stark reminder that for all the history we were soaking in, the present was just as raw and urgent.

Our differences came into sharp focus during the trip. Anand meticulously planned how we'd navigate security concerns, while I leaned into the spontaneity of the moment. He worried about what might go wrong, while I reveled in what was going right. And yet, in those moments of tension, we found balance.

Anand's vulnerability on this trip was new for me to witness. As someone who's usually so composed and logical, seeing him absorb the realities of Iraq—the shattered homes, the live bomb labeled "safe," the haunting silence of destruction—was humbling. For me, it reaffirmed the importance of holding on to what we cherish, of not taking anything for granted. For Anand, it was a lesson in seeing the world beyond the headlines and history books.

By the end of the trip, something had shifted between us. Anand may not have turned into a reckless adventurer overnight, but he saw the world a little more like I do: as a tapestry of stories waiting to be told, no matter how messy or uncomfortable they might be. And I saw the value in his caution, his ability to temper my wild impulses without stifling them.

Iraq taught us that opposites don't just attract—they complement, they challenge, and they grow together. And for all our differences, we left Iraq with a shared understanding: life's most extraordinary moments happen when you step out of your comfort zone—even if it takes a little convincing.

Baghdad

Baghdad. Once, it was called Madinat al-Salam—*the City of Peace.* I let the name roll off my tongue as we entered its bustling heart, feeling the poetic irony of it all. Today, the city is known more for conflict than for peace, but Baghdad's spirit isn't easily erased. Long before the world's gaze turned toward its scars, this was the center of the known universe—the glittering jewel of the Abbasid Caliphate, where scholars, poets, and explorers mingled in the golden glow of wisdom and art. It was here that the seeds of algebra were planted, where the stars were charted, and where stories like *One Thousand and One Nights* were born.

As our car weaved through the traffic, I couldn't help but feel the centuries of history—the very land where ancient empires once thrived: the Akkadians, the Babylonians, the Sumerians, and the Assyrians. It was a humbling thought, to imagine myself in a city that had shaped the course of human civilization.

"Can you believe we're walking on the same soil where Hammurabi's Code was written and where the Hanging Gardens might have once stood?" I asked my husband.

He glanced over, smiling at my enthusiasm. "Surreal, isn't it? It's like stepping into a living museum."

And it was. But instead of hushed corridors and glass cases, we were surrounded by the chaotic, vibrant pulse of everyday life. The Baghdad I had imagined was a city of soldiers and checkpoints, but the reality was strikingly different. Yes, there were signs of conflict, but they were overshadowed by something more profound—resilience. The city buzzed with honking cars, vendors shouting out their wares, and families gathering for their evening strolls. This was not a place of despair; it was a place of survival, of life stubbornly pushing through the cracks.

We paused at a small café on Al-Rasheed Street, a historic thoroughfare that once epitomized Baghdad's cosmopolitan spirit. The scent of *chai* filled the air, mingling with the aroma of fresh falafel and grilled kebabs. An elderly shopkeeper approached us with two steaming cups of tea, his eyes twinkling with curiosity.

"Where are you from?" he asked in halting English, setting the cups down before us.

"India," I replied, smiling.

His face lit up with recognition. "Hind!" he exclaimed, grinning broadly. Then, with a flourish, he added, "Amitabh Bachchan!" as if invoking a magical incantation.

I couldn't help but laugh, shaking my head. "If only you knew," I teased, "I'm more of a Rajinikanth fan."

The old man nodded approvingly, and we shared a moment of genuine laughter—a brief but meaningful connection that cut through any preconceived barriers. Interactions like these began to shift my perception of Baghdad. I had come expecting a city weighed down by war, but instead, I found it buoyed by the warmth of its people, their hospitality as vast as the desert that stretched beyond its borders.

Our first official stop was the Iraq Museum, an extraordinary archive of human history. Established in 1926, the museum houses artifacts from Mesopotamia, the "land between rivers," where civilization, as we know it, first took root. The air inside was cool, a welcome reprieve from the desert heat, and the silence felt almost sacred. I wandered through halls filled with ancient cuneiform tablets, delicate pottery, and the imposing stone statues of Sumerian kings. Each artifact told a story—a glimpse into a world that existed thousands of years before us.

I stopped in front of a small, intricately carved seal, its surface covered in a tiny, precise script. It was used for signing documents in the time of the Akkadian Empire, around 2300 BC. I traced the grooves with my eyes, imagining the hands that had held it, the deals that had been made, the lives that had played out in its presence.

Our next destination was Al-Mutanabbi Street, named after the great 10th-century poet who once declared, "I am the one whose literature can be seen by the blind and whose words are heard by the deaf." This street was Baghdad's literary soul, a haven for book lovers and intellectuals alike. The shops were stacked floor to ceiling with books—some new, others worn with the touch of countless hands. I picked up a volume of poetry, running my fingers over the Arabic script.

"Let's buy a few," I suggested, turning to my husband. "It feels like a small way to honor the legacy of this place."

He nodded, already thumbing through a collection of Sufi poetry, its pages whispering with ancient wisdom.

Just beyond the street, stood the Mustansiriyah Madrasa, one of the oldest universities in the world. Built in the 13th century, this institution was once a beacon of learning, where students came to study astronomy, medicine, and law. The intricate tilework still adorned its walls, though time had weathered much of its grandeur. Standing in its shadow,

I could almost hear the debates of scholars who once gathered here, discussing philosophy and science long before Europe's Renaissance had begun.

From there, we strolled toward Tahrir Square, where the sounds of the city converged in a symphony of life. This square, a symbol of resistance and revolution, had witnessed countless protests and movements, the voices of the people demanding change. The energy here was palpable, a reminder that Baghdad's story is far from over—it's still being written in the footsteps of those who gather here, in the dreams of children playing football in the streets.

As we approached Firdous Square, I couldn't help but recall the iconic images of Saddam Hussein's statue being toppled. Now, the empty pedestal stood as a silent witness to the passage of time, the void it left behind filled with the hopes of a city rebuilding itself piece by piece.

In the distance, the Martyrs Monument loomed against the skyline, its blue dome gleaming in the fading light. It stood as a testament to the resilience of the Iraqi people, a tribute to those who had given their lives in the Iran-Iraq War. The monument's striking form felt both sorrowful and triumphant, a symbol of a city that refuses to be defined by its tragedies.

As the sun dipped below the horizon, casting the city in shades of gold and shadow, I found myself thinking back to our trip to Damascus—a city I had once loved deeply. But Baghdad was different. It didn't invite romanticism or nostalgia. Instead, it demanded honesty. It laid itself bare, asking you to see it for what it truly was: a city scarred but not broken, ancient yet fiercely alive.

At that moment, I realized why I had come here. Not just to witness history, but to be part of it, if only for a brief while. Baghdad's story wasn't finished, and I was here to listen.

Babylon

The name itself feels like an incantation, summoning visions of grandeur and myth. In its heyday, this was the city of cities, the beating heart of ancient Mesopotamia—a place where Alexander the Great dreamt of creating a new world, where the mythical Hanging Gardens were said to have cascaded like waterfalls in the desert heat. As we stepped onto the dusty ruins of Babylon, I felt a shiver of anticipation. Here, the past doesn't just linger; it thrums like an ancient pulse beneath your feet.

We wandered deeper into the site. Our guide, a local historian with a deep, melodic voice, pointed out the foundations of what many believe to be the remnants of the Tower of Babel, the legendary ziggurat that once reached toward the heavens. Though its original height is lost to time and conquest, I could imagine the scholars debating philosophy, priests chanting hymns, and merchants haggling over precious goods. This was where humanity supposedly tried to bridge the gap between earth and sky, only for their languages to be scattered in divine disapproval.

“What do you think happened here?” I asked, my voice hushed as if I might disturb the ghosts of ancient conversations.

My husband glanced at the ruins, a playful smile tugging at his lips. “Probably some grand philosophical debates,” he mused. “Or maybe just a bunch of old men arguing over who could build it taller.”

We laughed, adding our own brief spark of life to this long-dead city. The laughter felt almost sacrilegious but also necessary—an offering to the silent, stoic walls that had witnessed so much over millennia.

We made our way toward a structure that stood out against the ancient landscape: Saddam Hussein’s summer palace, perched on a hill, looming like a brooding shadow over the ruins of Babylon. Its stark opulence felt like an affront to the subtle, worn beauty of the ancient city—a monument to ego built upon the bones of history. Here was a dictator’s attempt to insert himself into the narrative of Babylon’s glory, to claim a legacy he could never truly own.

“It’s surreal, isn’t it?” I remarked, staring up at the imposing structure. “To think of the parties and meetings that must have happened there, surrounded by the echoes of ancient civilizations.”

“Surreal and a bit obscene,” my husband added. “It feels like building a skyscraper in the middle of a desert oasis.”

The palace itself was a study in contradictions. We climbed the steps, entering what had once been a grand foyer, its walls adorned with Lebanese cedar wood, now faded and peeling. The air inside was still, heavy with the scent of abandonment. In the main conference room, the ceiling boasted an exquisitely painted mural—vibrant scenes of Babylonian life depicted in stunning detail: farmers harvesting grain, soldiers marching in formation, dancers performing beneath the moonlight. The artwork seemed almost alive, as if it was fighting against the decay that threatened to swallow it.

I stood beneath the mural, imagining the conversations that must have taken place here—decisions that would ripple across nations, whispered agreements sealed with handshakes and nods. I could almost picture Saddam himself, seated at the head of the table, surrounded by advisors, each decision heavy with the weight of power and paranoia.

"It's desolate now," my husband observed quietly, his voice softened by a sense of reverence.

I nodded, absorbing the stark emptiness of the room. The opulence had faded, leaving behind only traces of its former grandeur, like the ghost of a once-mighty ruler haunting his own palace. Outside, the sun had begun its slow descent, casting the ruins of Babylon in a golden, almost ethereal light.

We wandered back down the hill, away from the empty palace, and found ourselves once again among the ruins. I ran my fingers along the bricks of the Ishtar Gate, now restored and resplendent with its brilliant blue tiles. The gate once marked the grand entrance to Babylon, decorated with fierce lions and dragons that symbolized the might of the city. Standing here, I tried to picture the procession of soldiers and priests, the throngs of citizens who once gazed upon it in awe. The gate felt like a bridge between two worlds—the ancient and the modern, the forgotten and the remembered.

"Isn't it strange?" I said, looking back at the distant silhouette of the palace. "Babylon was once a symbol of civilization's peak, and now it's a ruin overshadowed by the ghost of a dictator's ambition."

My husband nodded, his gaze distant as he surveyed the landscape. "It's a powerful reminder that even the greatest empires fall, and even the most powerful leaders fade into obscurity."

At that moment, it struck me how both these sites—the magnificent, time-worn ruins of Babylon and the abandoned, hollow palace of Saddam—told stories intertwined with glory and decay, triumph and hubris. Here lay the remnants of humanity's greatest ambitions, bearing witness to the cyclical nature of power and legacy. It was a humbling thought, to stand between these two testaments of human history, feeling both the weight of our shared past and the fleeting nature of our present.

As we walked back toward our car, the sun dipped below the horizon, casting a deep, crimson glow over the plains of Mesopotamia. In that fading light, Babylon felt almost timeless, like a city suspended between its storied past and the uncertain future. It left me with a lingering sense of awe and melancholy—a reminder of the empires we build and the ruins we leave behind.

Najaf

Our journey to Najaf felt like stepping further into the soul of Iraq, a country that reveals itself slowly, like pages of an ancient manuscript worn at the edges. As we left behind the grandeur of Babylon, the landscape shifted—crumbling ruins gave way to a simpler, starker beauty. The plains stretched endlessly, dotted with small villages and clusters of date palms swaying under a cloudless sky. There was a quiet here that spoke of deep, unbroken traditions, anchored in faith and resilience.

Najaf was unlike any place we'd visited so far. Known as the heartland for *Shia* Islam, it held a profound spiritual significance, and the weight of that reverence pressed upon my chest as we approached the city's gates. There was an unspoken understanding between us—my husband's silent squeeze of my hand told me he felt it too. We were entering sacred ground.

When we arrived, the city was a swirl of contradictions—bustling markets alive with the shouts of vendors, and yet, an enveloping silence of unspoken prayers hung in the air. Men in traditional flowing robes hurried through the streets, their faces etched with purpose, while women clad in deep black abayas moved gracefully, their eyes holding stories I would never fully know. The shops were filled with religious artifacts: prayer beads glinting in the sunlight, intricate

Qur'anic calligraphy painted on ceramic plates, and small vials of rosewater, each drop a promise of blessings.

I hesitated before donning the burqa. The fabric felt heavy against my skin, but it was more than just clothing—it was a layer of respect, a way to honor the sanctity of this place and the people whose lives were woven into its fabric. I looked over at my husband, and his gentle nod reminded me why we were here: to understand, to bear witness, and to listen to the stories the stones couldn't tell.

The Imam Ali Mosque rose before us, its golden dome glinting in the midday sun like a beacon of hope. The very sight of it sent shivers down my spine. This was no ordinary structure; it was a spiritual epicenter, a place where millions of pilgrims had journeyed, seeking solace, redemption, or a chance to grieve. As we stepped into the vast courtyard, the mosaic tiles seemed to shimmer, casting a spell that quieted even the whispers of the wind.

The air was thick with the scent of incense and the soft murmur of prayers—a sound that resonated deep within me. I caught snippets of conversations, fragments of debates about faith and unity that felt timeless, as though these discussions had been taking place since the dawn of the city itself.

"Did you know Najaf isn't just a city? It's a sanctuary," a man said to his friend by the fountain, his voice tinged with both pride and sorrow. "It's where we honor Imam Ali's legacy. It's where our ancestors found refuge."

His companion nodded, a frown creasing his brow. "But outsiders see only our divisions. They don't understand the depth of our history, our struggles, or why this place matters."

Their words clung to me as we moved deeper into the mosque complex, weaving between clusters of pilgrims who had traveled from distant corners of the world. I saw tears of devotion streaming down weathered faces, hands reaching out to touch the cool marble pillars as though seeking an anchor for their grief. For a moment, I closed my eyes and let the energy of the place wash over me. It was overwhelming and humbling, a raw reminder of how faith can bind people together, even in the face of unimaginable loss.

In Najaf, I felt the echoes of ancient wounds, the scars left by sectarian violence that had marred Iraq's recent history. But there was also a palpable sense of hope—a collective longing for peace and understanding that transcended the divisions I had read about. This wasn't just a city steeped in religious significance; it was a testament to the resilience of its people, a symbol of their unyielding spirit.

Samarra and Hatra

Leaving behind the vibrant, spiritual pulse of Najaf, we drove north, the landscape gradually shifting once again. The road unfurled like a quiet promise, leading us into the open countryside toward Samarra. The journey felt like a meditation, the landscape shifting from arid plains to fertile fields where the green of life seemed to defy the sun's scorching embrace. In the distance, the Malwiya Minaret rose like a coiled serpent, its spiral form reaching for the heavens—a relic from a time when Samarra was a thriving capital of the Abbasid Caliphate.

Standing before the Malwiya Minaret, I marveled at its sheer scale and the ingenuity of its design. Built in the ninth century, it was inspired by the ziggurats of ancient Mesopotamia, a tribute to the civilizations that had laid the foundation for all that followed. I traced the path of the spiral walkway with my eyes, imagining the breathtaking views from the top—the vast expanse of Samarra's ruins, once teeming with scholars, merchants, and artists who had left their indelible mark on history.

But there was a heaviness here too, an unspoken grief that lingered like the dust stirred up by our footsteps. The destruction wrought by the Islamic State had left deep scars. I ran my fingers over the crumbling bricks, feeling the void where history had been stolen away, piece by piece. "It's heartbreaking," I whispered, unable to tear my eyes away from the shattered remnants of this once-great city.

My husband's voice broke the silence. "And yet, it's still standing," he said softly.

Our final stop was Hatra, a city that seemed to exist out of time, suspended between the past and the present. Walking through the grand entrance, I was struck by the fusion of Greco-Roman and Mesopotamian influences. The massive temple complex loomed before us, its columns carved with intricate designs that whispered of an era when Hatra was a thriving hub of trade and religion.

"This place is incredible," I breathed, taking in the sheer scale of the ruins.

"Imagine what it was like at its peak," my husband replied, his voice tinged with awe. "It must have been magnificent."

But even here, the shadows of recent destruction haunted us. Hatra, like Palmyra in Syria, had suffered under the hands of extremists. The ornate sculptures had been smashed, the intricate reliefs defaced—a deliberate attempt to erase a heritage that had withstood centuries of natural decay. I felt a wave of sadness wash over me, but also a fierce determination. These stones, worn by time and scarred by violence, were witnesses to human resilience, silent but unyielding.

Mosul

The scars of war ran deep through Mosul, leaving behind an eerie stillness that clung to the hollow shells of its once-bustling streets. I had read about Mosul's storied past, where Arabs, Kurds, and Turkmen lived side by side, their cultures intertwined. But standing here, it felt as though the threads had been violently severed, leaving only frayed remnants in their place.

"Look at that," I murmured, gesturing toward a crumbling structure that once stood proudly against the skyline.

My husband glanced over, his face shadowed with concern. "It's hard to believe this was once a thriving city," he said quietly, as if afraid to disturb the silence that lingered like a specter of the past.

We drove past the remnants of a world lost—whole blocks reduced to rubble, the ruins of what had once been homes, shops, and schools. The Grand Mosque of al-Nuri, once an emblem of Mosul's architectural splendor with its iconic leaning minaret, now lay in ruins—a hollow shell, stripped of its former glory. I felt a pang of sadness as I imagined the prayers that had once echoed through its halls, now replaced by the empty whisper of wind through broken walls.

"Mosul was a trade hub for centuries," I reflected aloud, trying to picture the city in its prime. "Its strategic location connected cultures and economies from across the region."

He nodded. "Now it feels like all that's left is the pain."

It was impossible not to feel the weight of loss in the air. The people of Mosul, who had borne witness to centuries of history, now carried the collective memory of a city brought to its knees in mere moments. We moved slowly through streets lined with half-standing buildings, each one an unsettling monument to what had once been a vibrant, living place.

"We should find someone to talk to," I suggested in my hushed voice. "Someone who can tell us what it's like now, beyond the rubble."

As if summoned by my words, we spotted an elderly man seated on a worn stool outside what remained of his shop. His gaze swept over the devastation, but there was something in his eyes—a flicker of resilience, a quiet defiance against the destruction that surrounded him.

"Excuse me," I approached cautiously. "Could you tell us about Mosul?"

He looked up slowly, his eyes meeting mine with a depth that held decades of stories untold. His face, weathered by time and hardship, softened as he began to speak.

"This city is my life," he said. "I've seen it flourish, and I've seen it fall apart."

There was a fondness in his voice, a love for a place that had been a sanctuary for so many, long before conflict had cast its shadow over the land.

"But we will rebuild," he said, and there was a quiet conviction in his words. "This land has seen worse. It will see better again."

In his voice, I heard a truth that cut through the rubble: this was about more than restoring buildings. It was about reclaiming identity, preserving culture, and reviving the soul of a city. Despite everything, there was hope—fragile, but present. His words stayed with me long after we left, a reminder that even in the face of unimaginable loss, the human spirit can find a way to endure, to rebuild, and to remember.

Kurdistan

Crossing the border into Iraqi Kurdistan felt like stepping through a portal into another world—a stark and thrilling contrast from the desolate ruins of Mosul left behind.

The landscape transformed almost instantly, from the remnants of a war-ravaged cityscape to a vista of rolling, verdant hills blanketed with wildflowers. Their vibrant petals danced like colorful confetti tossed by a benevolent breeze, offering a kaleidoscope of life that defied the bleak, war-torn narrative so often depicted by the media. This was Kurdistan as few outsiders ever saw it: a hidden gem, vibrant and untamed, whispering of ancient histories and untold stories.

I took a deep breath, savoring the crisp, clean air tinged with the sweet scent of blooming flora and fresh earth. It was as though the land itself was breathing, inviting us to immerse ourselves in its lush embrace. Villages dotted the horizon like strokes of paint on a pastoral canvas—stone houses blending seamlessly into the verdant hillsides, their modest beauty a testament to the harmony between human habitation and nature's bounty. It felt surreal, like stepping into a postcard where life moved at a gentler, more deliberate pace.

"Look at that," I said, pointing to a cluster of homes perched precariously on a steep mountainside, each one a silent keeper of countless untold stories.

My husband turned to look, his eyes sparkling with the same sense of wonder that filled my own. "It's incredible," he murmured, as if afraid his voice might shatter the enchantment of the moment.

Our first stop was Erbil, the vibrant heart of Kurdistan and one of the oldest continuously inhabited cities in the world. The ancient citadel loomed above us, a majestic fortress guarding centuries of history, its weathered stones imbued with the memories of countless generations.

"Try this," I urged my husband, handing him a piece of baklava glistening with honey.

He took a bite, his face lighting up in delight as he savored the rich, nutty sweetness. "This is amazing," he exclaimed, his enthusiasm contagious. We shared a smile, feeling a profound connection not just to each other, but to this ancient land that had witnessed so many before us savoring similar moments of joy.

Beyond the city, the countryside beckoned with its own treasures. We drove past signs pointing toward Shanidar Cave, an archaeological site that had once been home to Neanderthals. The thought stirred my imagination, and I found myself picturing those early humans huddled around fires under a starlit sky, crafting tools and sharing stories of their own.

"What do you think they lived like?" I mused, the question hanging in the air as we passed the rugged cliffs leading up to the cave.

"Survival must have been their main focus," my husband replied. "But imagine what it would have been like, forging a life in a place like this."

I could almost see it—their laughter mingling with the crackle of flames, the smell of roasting meat filling the night air.

Our journey took us next to the Rabban Hormizd Monastery, an ancient sanctuary perched high on a rocky hill, like a vigilant guardian overlooking the sprawling valleys below. The climb left us breathless—not just from the effort, but from the sheer beauty that unfolded with every step. The view was a masterpiece painted by nature herself: lush green valleys stretched out in all directions, kissed by sunlight that turned the landscape into a mosaic of gold and emerald.

We made our way to Lalish, the spiritual heart of the Yazidi community, where the warmth of its people enveloped us like a comforting embrace. It was a sacred space, the kind where the walls themselves seemed to hum with the energy of countless prayers. We were welcomed with open arms and genuine smiles. Their hospitality was a powerful antidote to the fear and misunderstanding often associated with this region.

"This place is special," my husband remarked softly as we listened to the stories shared by our hosts. They spoke of ancient traditions, passed down through generations. In their words, I found a powerful lesson about the resilience of the human spirit—how it can thrive in harmony amidst diversity, defying the simplistic, reductive labels imposed by the outside world.

Our path led us further into the Kurdish countryside, through the rugged beauty of Rawanduz and Akre, where every twist in the road revealed another breathtaking vista. We marvelled at the sight of waterfalls cascading down jagged cliffs, their waters sparkling in the sunlight like strands of silver. The quaint mountain towns seemed to whisper secrets from ages past, inviting us to explore their cobbled streets and hidden corners.

Over the three days we spent traversing the Kurdish landscape, I felt a deepening connection to this place. Here, the past did not linger as a ghostly shadow but thrived as a living, breathing part of the present that I was grateful to witness and become a small part of.

Iraq, Beyond the Headlines

I wanted to stand atop every minaret, every ancient ziggurat, and shout for the world to hear: *Iraq is so much more than its struggles!*

One evening, as we sat beneath a sky awash with stars, I turned to my husband. "Traveling here," I said, my voice tinged with awe, "has shown me that beauty can not only survive but *thrive* in the face of adversity."

He nodded, his gaze fixed on the shimmering canvas above us. "There's a depth here," he agreed quietly, "a richness that goes far beyond what the news ever captures."

If you're considering a journey to Iraq, I urge you: don't let fear or preconceived notions hold you back. Yes, safety must be your first priority—stay informed, research thoroughly, and heed travel advisories. But if you're willing to venture beyond the familiar comfort zones of typical tourist destinations, Iraq offers experiences that are unparalleled in their depth and meaning.

This isn't a place for the faint of heart or for those who seek a packaged, sanitized vacation. It's for the curious, the intrepid, the ones who long to step into the pages of history and feel the pulse of a land that has been a crossroads of cultures for millennia. Pack lightly, but pack wisely. Bring sturdy, comfortable shoes—they'll be your best companion as you tread through the ruins of Babylon, where Nebuchadnezzar once ruled, or the sun-bleached stones of Hatra, a testament to ancient civilizations that once thrived in the desert heat.

Carry a journal; you'll want to document every detail, every unexpected moment of connection. The stories you'll gather won't just be about the places you see but about the people you meet—the old shopkeeper in Mosul who offers you a piece of sweet baklava with a smile that feels like a gift, the young Kurdish guide in Erbil who proudly shares his culture over cups of tea that taste like liquid sunshine.

Learn a few phrases in Arabic or Kurdish; even the simplest greetings will break barriers and light up faces. Respect the customs of this land when you visit its sacred sites—dress modestly and tread lightly, for these are places steeped in tradition, places where the air feels thick with prayers whispered over centuries.

Iraq's landscapes will leave you breathless: from the sweeping golden deserts that whisper tales of ancient caravans to the verdant hills of Kurdistan, where wildflowers bloom defiantly in every hue imaginable. The country's rugged mountain passes offer road trips with views that rival the most celebrated scenic routes of the world, while its rivers, the Tigris and the Euphrates, flow with stories that date back to the dawn of time.

Why not trade in the predictability of a European vacation for the raw, unfiltered beauty of Iraq? Why not allow this ancient land to challenge you, to push the boundaries of your comfort and your understanding? Let Iraq surprise you, as it did me. Let its charm seep into your bones, its stories settle into the corners of your heart, and its people teach you about resilience, hospitality, and the unbreakable spirit of a place that has seen so much, endured so much, and still stands proud.

Iraq deserves a spot on every traveler's bucket list—not just for its history, but for the future it is still writing. This journey is not merely about seeing ancient ruins or ticking off destinations; it's about bearing witness to a living, breathing narrative that transcends time, borders, and belief systems. It's about connecting with a part of the world that, despite all its scars, remains deeply, achingly beautiful.

So, go ahead. Step off the beaten path. Say yes to the unknown. And trust me—when you find yourself standing amidst the sunlit ruins of Babylon or looking out over the lush valleys of Kurdistan, you'll realize that this journey was worth every moment of doubt. Let Iraq's stories become part of your own; let its spirit inspire your travels for years to come.

Chapter V

HORMUZ ISLAND, IRAN

August 2022

> ***I will not have my life narrowed down. I will not bow down to somebody else's whim or to someone else's ignorance.***
>
> ***– Bell Hooks***

If you've ever dreamed of walking on Mars, Hormuz Island might be the closest you'll come without leaving Earth. It's truly the Rainbow Treasure of Iran. A tiny speck in the Persian Gulf, just eight kilometers off the southern coast of Iran, Hormuz is an island that defies imagination. It's a kaleidoscope of raw, unfiltered nature—a surreal landscape painted in vivid reds, golds, and purples by the mineral-rich soils and salt deposits that have sculpted its terrain over millennia. Known as the *Rainbow Island*, Hormuz is more than just a visual spectacle. It's a place where history, culture, and geology collide in the most unexpected ways.

Hormuz has played a pivotal role in world history, once standing as a linchpin in the maritime trade routes of the Persian Empire. It was a bustling hub, trading spices, silk, and precious goods between Asia, the Middle East, and Europe. Today, it feels like a hidden corner of the world, far removed from the modern hustle—an artist's canvas untouched by time.

Stepping off the boat that ferried me across the shimmering waters from Bandar Abbas, I felt like I'd arrived in a parallel universe. The sand beneath my feet was a vibrant rust red, a hue so startling it seemed as though the earth itself had bled color. Above me, the sky stretched endlessly, a deep cobalt blue that framed the island like a dome. To my right, cliffs rose in dramatic waves of orange and yellow, their surfaces cracked and rippled as if shaped by an unseen artist's hand.

I stood there, at the edge of Hormuz Island, letting the warm Persian Gulf breeze weave through my hair, as I gazed at the turquoise expanse before me. Behind me, once again, the island sprawled like a painter's palette—vivid strokes of reds, yellows, purples, and ochres sprawled across its rugged terrain. This tiny haven, tucked within the Hormozgan Province of southern Iran, is a marvel of geological artistry, shaped by the whispers of time and the quietude of isolation.

"Welcome to Hormuz," a soft yet commanding voice interrupted my reverie. Turning, I saw Leila, my guide for this journey. Her eyes sparkled with the pride of someone whose roots run deep in this land. Leila embodied the soul of Hormuz itself—graceful, resilient, and layered with stories waiting to be uncovered.

As we began our trek along a trail bordered by wildflowers, Leila shared how Hormuz often escapes the itineraries of tourists. "Most people head straight to Shiraz or Tehran. They don't realize that places like this hold the magic they're searching for," she said with a wry smile.

Her words rang true as we arrived at a bustling village market. Women dressed in bright, flowing fabrics haggled over fresh produce, their faces lit with unguarded smiles.

"What do you think?" Leila asked, handing me a piece of freshly baked bread slathered in honey.

"It's incredible," I replied, savoring the sweet, earthy flavors. "It feels alive."

Hormuz Island has always been alive, not only with the resilience of its people but also with the pulse of history. Once a linchpin in the ancient trade routes, Hormuz was a thriving port in the 14th century, its shores a meeting place for merchants from India, China, and Europe. The Portuguese briefly occupied it in the 16th century, leaving behind fortresses whose crumbling walls still whisper tales of conflict and commerce.

Leila and I ventured deeper into the island's interior, where nature had truly outdone itself. Hormuz is not merely land; it's a canvas. We climbed to a viewpoint overlooking Rainbow Valley, where hills shimmered in surreal hues of red, gold, and lavender. She scooped up a handful of crimson sand, letting the iron-rich grains slip through her fingers. "This is *gelak*," she explained. "We use it in art, food, and even for rituals. It's part of who we are."

In another valley, jagged rocks sculpted by millennia of wind resembled mythical creatures frozen in time. "These are the Valley of Statues," Leila said as we wandered among the surreal formations. Each corner of the island seemed to tell its own story, inviting me to pause and listen.

At the aptly named Purple Beach, manganese-rich sands sparkled under the sun as waves gently lapped at the shore. It was as if nature had hidden pieces of treasure all over Hormuz, waiting for the curious to uncover them.

While Hormuz offered wonder at every turn, Leila didn't shy away from the challenges faced by women travelers in Iran. "Simple freedoms like walking alone or speaking openly in public can feel restricted," she admitted, her expression momentarily clouded. Yet Leila herself was navigating the nuances of tradition and progressing with grace. As a guide, she ensured I felt safe and respected while encouraging me to immerse myself fully in Hormuz's culture and rhythm. Her candidness deepened my appreciation for the island—not as a mere destination but as a microcosm of a world grappling with the interplay between heritage and modernity.

On our final day, we sat on a cliff overlooking the Strait of Hormuz, where the Gulf's shimmering waters merged into the Arabian Sea. It was hard to reconcile the tranquility of the view with the strait's reputation as one of the world's most strategically important waterways. Around 20% of global oil passes through this narrow passage—a stark reminder of the contrasts that define Hormuz. Leila broke the silence.

"This place isn't just beautiful," she said. "It has a soul. It challenges you, welcomes you, and changes you."

A Journey Through Nature's Masterpiece

The next morning, the first blush of dawn illuminated Bandar Abbas, casting its soft hues over the bustling port. My small, rickety boat bobbed on the water, its aging wood creaking with each gentle wave. The air was crisp, tinged with salt and the faint aroma of freshly caught fish from nearby markets. As the boat's engine hummed to life, I felt a palpable sense of anticipation. Hormuz Island awaited—a place whispered about in traveler's tales as both a geologist's dream and an artist's muse.

The journey itself was a precursor to the marvels ahead. The turquoise waters of the Persian Gulf stretched endlessly, the horizon shimmering like molten glass under the rising sun. Seagulls trailed our boat, their cries mingling with the rhythmic slap of waves. Slowly, the island emerged from the mist—a bold, colorful silhouette rising defiantly from the sea. When we docked, the island welcomed us with a kaleidoscope of colors. Vibrant reds, ochres, and shimmering silvers painted the landscape like a canvas come to life. Leila was already waiting, her smile as warm as the morning sun. "Let's start with the Goddess of Salt," she said, leading me along a dusty trail flanked by scrubby vegetation. The path wound through an ever-changing palette, with hues shifting subtly as we walked. It was as if the earth itself was alive, breathing and pulsating with energy. Arriving at the Goddess of Salt, I stopped in awe. Towering salt formations jutted from the ground like a frozen ocean, waves crystallized mid-motion. The cliffs glimmered in the sunlight, their pristine white surfaces etched with delicate patterns shaped by wind and water over millennia.

"Legend says she protects the island," Leila explained, her voice almost reverent. I reached out, tracing the cool, crystalline edges of the salt structures, marveling at their intricate beauty. They sparkled like gemstones under the sun, each one unique and unyielding. As we continued, the landscape transformed again, leading us to the famed Rainbow Mountain Valley. The first glimpse took my breath away—a symphony of colors rippling across the terrain, from fiery reds and burnt oranges to soothing purples and greens. The layers told a story of volcanic upheavals and the slow dance of time.

"Doesn't it feel like you're walking through a painting?" I asked Leila, unable to suppress my wonder.

She laughed. "It does. But here, the artist is the earth itself."

The Valley of Statues was our next stop—a surreal, almost eerie expanse where towering rock formations stood like sentinels guarding a forgotten kingdom. Each formation bore a distinct shape, resembling animals, mythical creatures, and even human figures.

"It's said that the wind whispers secrets here," Leila mused, her voice tinged with mystery. As the breeze picked up, I almost believed her. The statues seemed alive, their weathered surfaces telling tales of ancient winds and waters that had shaped them over eons.

From there, we ventured into the Colorful Cave, a hidden gem that felt like stepping into a secret realm. Inside, the walls gleamed with vibrant streaks of minerals—turquoises, pinks, and deep oranges swirled together in dazzling patterns. The air was cool and damp, and the cave seemed to hum with an energy that defied description.

"It's like walking inside a gemstone," I said.

Leila nodded. "Hormuz holds surprises in every corner."

Yet nothing prepared me for the spellbinding beauty of Red-Silver Beach. The sand glowed with a deep crimson hue, interspersed with glistening streaks of silver. Kneeling down, I let the grains slip through my fingers, the rich red staining my skin like henna.

"It's iron oxide," Leila explained. "The locals call it 'blood sand.'"

The contrast between the vivid sand and the gentle blue waves created an almost ethereal scene. Here, the past and present seemed to converge—the sands holding secrets of ancient rituals and geological marvels.

At Turtle Beach, tranquility reigned. The soft sands bore delicate tracks where sea turtles had made their nightly pilgrimage to nest. The air was thick with the earthy scent of nearby mangroves, and the rhythmic lapping of waves provided a soothing backdrop. It felt as though time had slowed, allowing me to absorb every detail of this untouched paradise.

Our final stop was Saffron Beach, where the shoreline shimmered with golden hues. Salt crystals formed intricate patterns beneath the shallow waters, catching the sunlight in a way that made the beach seem like it was woven from strands of gold.

Over the next three days, Hormuz revealed itself in layers, each more captivating than the last. From the surreal landscapes to the warm hospitality of its people, the island left an indelible mark on my soul. It was a reminder that true adventure isn't just about discovering new places—it's about connecting with the essence of those places, allowing them to change you in ways you never imagined.

Damash Siahoo Valley

On my final morning in Hormozgan, the call of adventure pulled me toward Damash Siahoo Valley—a hidden Eden that seemed too magical to be real. It was the kind of place that sounded like a travel rumor, the kind you hear about from a friend of a friend and immediately Google to see if it's real. And let me tell you: it's real, and it's everything. The drive alone was a feast for the eyes. Winding roads snaked through verdant hillsides, each turn unveiling scenes more luscious than the last. Ferns and wildflowers spilled onto the pavement like nature couldn't quite contain itself.

I leaned out of the car window, letting the wind whip through my hair, a giddy grin plastered across my face.

"This is insane!" I shouted over the sound of the engine, my excitement bubbling over like uncorked champagne.

Leila laughed, her own eyes sparkling with the same thrill. "Wait till you see the valley. This is just the prelude!"

And oh, what a main act it was. The valley spread out before us like a green-and-gold quilt stitched together by the hands of some whimsical deity. Tall palms waved lazily in the breeze, and crystal-clear water snaked through the lush vegetation, glinting under the sun like liquid sapphire. It was so postcard-perfect that I half-expected a unicorn to saunter into view.

Our guides, a pair of jovial locals with sun-kissed skin and easy smiles, led us to a canoe bobbing gently on the water. "Hop in," one said, gesturing like he was inviting us to a VIP ride through paradise.

The canoe glided through the water with a hypnotic rhythm, the paddles slicing the surface like whispers. Below us, fish darted like living streaks of silver, while the valley wrapped around us in a cozy, emerald embrace. Birds chirped high above, their songs echoing like nature's playlist.

At one point, the guides steered us toward a secluded cove, where the water kissed a tiny beach tucked between towering cliffs. The sand was so white it hurt my eyes, and the gentle waves rolled in like they were trying not to disturb the serenity.

"Should we stop here?" Leila asked, already halfway out of the canoe. "Um, is that even a question?" I said, kicking off my shoes and wading into the cool, glassy water. We spent the next hour swimming, laughing, and generally acting like we were on the set of some surreal nature documentary. The water was so clear I could see every pebble beneath my feet, each one polished smooth by years of gentle currents. Time slipped away as we floated on our backs, staring up at a sky so blue it felt like a portal to another dimension.

Eventually, hunger lured us back to shore, where our guides had set up a picnic under the shade of a sprawling palm tree. The spread was simple yet perfect: saffron-scented rice, roasted eggplants slick with olive oil, and flatbread so fresh it practically steamed in my hands. Every bite was bursting with flavors that somehow tasted like the land itself—earthy, vibrant, and alive.

"I don't think I've ever been this happy," I confessed between mouthfuls, my legs stretched out on the soft grass. "Same," Leila said, raising her tin cup of tea in a toast. "To Damash Siahoo—the valley that stole our hearts!"

But the day wasn't over yet. After lunch, we set off on foot to explore the valley's wilder corners. The air grew thick with the intoxicating scent of wild jasmine and damp earth, and the trails were flanked by ferns so tall they brushed against our arms as we walked. Butterflies flitted past in a kaleidoscope of colors, their delicate wings catching the sunlight like shards of stained glass.

Every turn brought a new marvel—a hidden waterfall cascading into a pool so blue it felt otherworldly, a grove of ancient trees that seemed to hum with secrets, and clusters of wildflowers so bright they looked like they'd been plugged into an electric socket. It was as if the valley was showing off, eager to reveal every treasure it had been hiding for centuries.

By the time we made our way back to the car, the sun was dipping low, casting the valley in a golden glow that felt almost holy. I looked back one last time, committing every detail to memory. Damash Siahoo wasn't just a place; it was a feeling—a heady cocktail of wonder, peace, and the kind of joy that comes from being utterly present in the moment.

As we drove away, I couldn't shake the thought that I'd just experienced something truly rare: a slice of the world that felt untouched by time, a paradise that hadn't yet been claimed by the chaos of modern life. And in that moment, I promised myself I'd return one day—not just to see it again, but to feel it, to let it remind me of the beauty that exists when you slow down and let nature work its magic.

Iran Reimagined

Newsflash: Iran has islands—and they are *straight-up spectacular.*

Forget what you think you know about this country, because Hormuz Island isn't just a place; it's an experience, a living canvas of wild beauty that refuses to be boxed into clichés. Picture this: mangrove forests tangled with secrets, deserts shimmering like gold, mountains painted in technicolor dreams, and beaches so empty they feel like they belong to you and only you. Sounds unreal? Trust me, it's very real—and it's waiting for you to show up.

When I first set foot on Hormuz, I was buzzing with the kind of anticipation you get before a blind date with someone wildly out of your league. But there was also a bittersweet pang in my chest. This was Iran—a country brimming with natural and cultural treasures, yet tangled in the weight of its current struggles. I'd arrived just weeks before protests ignited across the nation, and many of the women I met spoke openly about the frustrations they carried.

"Do you mind wearing the scarf?" one of them asked me, her gaze searching. I hesitated before answering honestly. As a traveler, I didn't mind—it felt like a small trade-off for the opportunity to explore this incredible land. But I also knew my privilege; I'd be leaving soon, returning to a life where wearing—or not wearing—something was my choice.

That duality clung to me throughout my visit: the beauty of Hormuz's and the stories of the resilient people who call this place home.

Here's the thing the headlines won't tell you: Iran is an *absolute vibe* for the adventurous traveler. It's safe. It's affordable. And it's brimming with the kind of hospitality that makes you feel like a long-lost cousin at a family reunion. Growing up in the Middle East, I've seen my share of jaw-dropping landscapes, but Hormuz left me starry-eyed. It's not just the vistas—it's the way the land feels alive, pulsing with a raw energy that seeps into your soul.

Hormuz isn't about manicured tourist spots or picture-perfect itineraries. It's about finding yourself ankle-deep in salt flats that look like lunar terrain, eating saffron-infused dishes with locals who treat you like royalty, and chasing sunsets that set the horizon on fire. It's the kind of place where nature and culture swirl together in a way that makes you forget the world you left behind.

If you're tired of cookie-cutter travel plans and Instagram hotspots that feel as hollow as they look, let Hormuz shake you up.

Iran, and Hormuz in particular, isn't just a destination. It's a story, one you get to write yourself. Forget the headlines, forget the stereotypes. Go. Feel. Explore. Because here's the secret: the world isn't waiting to be understood—it's waiting to be experienced. And Hormuz Island is calling. Answer it.

Getting to Hormuz Island

If Hormuz Island is calling your name, let me arm you with everything you need to make the journey seamless and spectacular. Your adventure begins in Bandar Abbas, a bustling port city in southern Iran. Flights to Bandar Abbas are available from major cities like Tehran, Shiraz, or Isfahan, and the journey offers a scenic preview of Iran's diverse landscapes. If you're already in the Gulf region, check for regional flights that might bring you even closer.

From Bandar Abbas, hop on a ferry to Hormuz Island. Ferries operate several times a day, and the ride takes just about 30-40 minutes. Pro tip: snag a seat on the upper deck to soak in the views of the sparkling Persian Gulf. Keep your camera ready—you'll want to capture those first glimpses of Hormuz's vivid coastline.

Visa Requirements

Iran offers a visa-on-arrival (VOA) for travelers from many countries. However, always check the latest requirements specific to your nationality. Make sure your passport is valid for at least six months and have your travel insurance and a copy of your accommodation booking handy—they may ask for these at immigration.

What to Pack

- Comfortable clothing: Lightweight, breathable layers are your best friend, but remember to respect local dress codes. Women should pack a scarf to cover their hair and loose clothing that covers arms and legs. Men should avoid shorts and sleeveless tops.

- Sturdy shoes: The island's terrain is diverse—you'll encounter beaches, rocky paths, and salt flats, so bring shoes that can handle it all.

- Sun protection: Sunscreen, sunglasses, and a hat are essentials. The island's sun doesn't mess around.

- Reusable water bottle: Hydration is key, and carrying your own bottle helps reduce plastic waste.

Where to Stay

Hormuz Island doesn't boast luxury resorts, but that's part of its charm. You'll find cozy guesthouses run by locals who are happy to share their culture and stories. Homestays are a fantastic way to connect with the community and get a taste of authentic Iranian hospitality.

For a unique experience, consider camping. The island's surreal landscapes make it an unforgettable spot for stargazing. There are no official campsites, but you can pitch a tent along the beaches. Just ensure you leave no trace behind—Hormuz's pristine beauty deserves our respect.

Local Delights

Don't leave without tasting *ghaliyeh mahi*, a fragrant fish stew that's a staple of the region, or *ranginak*, a sweet treat made from dates, walnuts, and spices. The island's cuisine is a blend of Persian and coastal flavors, offering a culinary adventure to match its landscapes.

Basic Facts to Fuel Your Curiosity

- Hormuz Island is known as the "Rainbow Island" due to its colorful mountains and striking landscapes, rich in red ochre and other minerals.

- The island is small—around 42 square kilometers—making it perfect for exploring on foot, by bike, or with a local tuk-tuk.
- Hormuz's soil isn't just beautiful; it's unique. Locals even use it as a spice in traditional dishes! The island's red soil, known as Golak, is a natural wonder in itself.
- Wildlife enthusiasts can spot dolphins, sea turtles, and a variety of birds along the coast.

Final Tips

- Respect the environment: Hormuz Island thrives on its untouched beauty. Avoid littering, and be mindful of the delicate ecosystems.
- Cash is king: While larger cities in Iran may accept cards, Hormuz is a cash-only zone. Bring Iranian rials, as there are no ATMs on the island.
- Stay connected: Internet access can be patchy, so download maps and travel guides ahead of time.

WILD AND RAW

In the wilderness, where the raw and wild intersect, lies the essence of untamed beauty and pure freedom.

Tales of Congo | Madagascar | Gabon | South Sudan

Chapter VI

DEMOCRATIC REPUBLIC OF CONGO

August 2023

> ***When you feel the tug of the wild, listen—it's the voice of something ancient calling you home.***
>
> ***– Jane Goodall***

Wild and Raw. There's something about these words that stirs a primal yearning. They conjure images of untouched wilderness, the kind that speaks in whispers and roars, beckoning you to step beyond the comforts of the known. The Democratic Republic of Congo, the first chapter in this category, is the very embodiment of wild and raw—a place that refuses to be tamed, demanding to be experienced on its own terms.

Nestled in the heart of Central Africa, the DRC is a land of contrasts, its vastness stretching across more than 2.3 million square kilometers, making it the second-largest country on the continent. With Kinshasa as its bustling capital—a city of over 17 million people, pulsating with life—it feels almost paradoxical that just beyond the urban sprawl lies one of the world's last true wildernesses.

Congo is home to over 100 million people who speak a rich tapestry of languages. *Lingala, Swahili, Kikongo,* and *Tshiluba* are the country's national languages, threading together a population that's as diverse as the landscapes they inhabit. French, a relic of its colonial past, serves as the *lingua franca*, uniting voices from sprawling cities to remote villages.

Before I even set foot on its soil, the Democratic Republic of Congo had already taken root in my imagination—a labyrinth of dense rainforests, murmuring rivers, and shadowed trails where life unfolds in ways both ancient and untamed. As the plane descended into Kinshasa, I felt a pull deep within, as if the land itself was summoning me, daring me to come closer, to listen to its heartbeat. This was a place where time didn't merely pass; it draped itself over the land, thick and languorous, entwined with the vines and the lives they cradled.

My journey began in the embrace of the Congo Basin, an emerald world that stretched beyond the horizon. Towering trees arched like cathedral spires above me, their leaves whispering a language older than words.

I had come to Congo chasing the echoes of its incredible biodiversity, but it was more than scientific curiosity that led me here. This was a pilgrimage, a quest to encounter the soul of a place that holds one of Earth's greatest treasures: its rainforests. These sprawling, pulsating lungs of the planet were a world unto themselves, sheltering creatures that felt like mythical beings come to life.

The gorillas were what drew me in most fiercely. I'd seen them before, in Uganda's Bwindi Impenetrable Forest, but the thought of meeting them again in Congo stirred the same breathless anticipation. Gorillas, with their dark, soulful eyes, seemed to hold a mirror to humanity—reminding us of what we share and what we stand to lose. Yet, Congo was not just about its iconic wildlife. It was the Okapi, slipping like a whispered secret through the underbrush; the countless birds, their plumage a kaleidoscope of impossible hues; and the hidden creatures whose names I might never know, but whose existence enriched this lush, breathing masterpiece. Every step I took deeper into the forest was a step away from the known and toward something elemental. The guide, Emmanuel, one of the guardians of this sanctuary, spoke of his land with reverence while I added, "Did you know that Congo is one of the most biodiverse places on the planet?" Did you know the Congo River is the deepest river in the world? This river, the second longest in Africa, wasn't just a geographical marvel; it was the lifeblood of the country. Flowing through the equator, the Congo River Basin feeds the world's second-largest rainforest, a lush expanse that regulates the Earth's climate. To trek through its dense foliage is to step into the lungs of the planet.

"Here," one said, his voice firm yet tender, "we live by nature's rhythm. To protect it is to protect ourselves."

His words were an anchor in a world that could easily sweep you away. The Congo wasn't just about conservation; it was about connection—between people and their environment, between the past and the promise of tomorrow.

As I pushed further into the rainforest, I realized that this journey was far more than an escape. It was an invitation to witness the power of a landscape that defies categorization, a land alive with its own heartbeat. Congo wasn't asking to be explored; it was asking to be understood. And as I stood beneath its ancient canopy, I felt ready to listen.

Tchegera Island

Pronounced *"Cheh-geh-rah,"* Tchegera Island revealed itself as the boat skimmed across the glimmering expanse of Lake Kivu. The water shimmered in shades of sapphire and jade, shifting with the play of sunlight. Each wave, kissed by light, sparkled like scattered diamonds, as if guarding ancient secrets within its depths. As we glided through the lake's gentle ripples, the mist began to lift, unveiling the island's crescent-shaped silhouette—a serene haven emerging from the water like a dream made real.

This volcanic island is part of the Democratic Republic of Congo's Virunga National Park, a region celebrated for its pristine beauty and vibrant ecosystems.

The scent of the lake—fresh and faintly mineral—mingled with the earthy aroma of the dense greenery that crowned the island. As we neared the shore, the landscape became vivid with lush forests cascading down to meet sandy beaches, their emerald tones punctuated by bursts of fiery reds and yellows from the wildflowers. Even from the boat, I could hear the island alive with sound—chirping birds, the occasional rustle of wind through the trees, and the gentle rhythm of waves greeting the shore.

Stepping onto the sand, soft and warm underfoot, was like crossing into a world suspended in time. The lake's waters kissed the beach gently, their turquoise hues reflecting the sky. My guide, a tall, steady man with an easy smile, gestured toward a cluster of palms swaying in the breeze.

"Look at that view!" I exclaimed.

He nodded knowingly, pointing toward a rocky outcrop that jutted out into the lake. "This place," he said, "is for those who seek peace. Many come here just to be still." I followed his gaze to where the clear waters hugged the rocky edges of the island, shimmering like liquid glass. Behind us, the hills rose dramatically, their slopes draped in dense vegetation. The horizon ahead stretched endlessly, where the lake and sky fused into a serene blur of blue. This was tranquility in its purest form. Venturing inland, I found myself immersed in a symphony of life. Tall grasses brushed against my arms as I walked, and the vibrant calls of exotic birds filled the air. Occasionally, a flash of color darted across the undergrowth—a kingfisher perhaps, or another feathered jewel native to this region.

"Do you know why Tchegera is shaped like this?" my guide asked suddenly. "It's a remnant of a collapsed volcanic caldera. What you see now is what remains of the rim."

Nature's resilience astounded me. Here was an island born from fire and destruction, yet it now thrived with life. In a quiet corner of the island, I stumbled upon a secluded cove where tiny fish darted between smooth stones, their scales catching the light like living rainbows. A fallen tree nearby had transformed into a canvas for nature's artists—fungi in hues of orange and green fanned out like intricate lace.

"Mama Africa shows her beauty here," I murmured under my breath, entranced by the perfection of the scene.

My guide smiled at my words, his pride unmistakable. "This is a gift," he said simply, gesturing at the landscape around us. Deeper still, the island revealed another secret: a small clearing where wildflowers swayed in the gentle breeze. Their petals, impossibly delicate, formed patterns so intricate they could only have been crafted by nature's hand. I knelt to touch one, careful not to disturb its fragile grace.

Gorilla Encounters

The morning began before the sun had risen, the air buzzing with quiet energy and the thrill of expectation. Today was more than an adventure—it was a pilgrimage into the untamed world of mountain gorillas. As the first streaks of light painted the horizon, I laced up my boots and adjusted my backpack. The journey ahead promised to test both my endurance and my spirit.

By a little past 7 a.m., I stood at the edge of the national park, where sunlight streamed through the canopy in golden shafts, casting an ethereal glow on the forest floor. Every breath was heavy with moisture, tinged with the scents of damp earth and blossoming greenery. Around me, the jungle hummed with life—a chorus of chirping birds, buzzing insects, and the occasional rustle of unseen creatures.

Mosi, my guide, moved with the surety of someone who had walked these paths for nearly two decades. His presence was reassuring, a living link between this raw, unpredictable wilderness and my cautious steps. "Keep your eyes open and your steps light," he said with a grin, his voice carrying a note of excitement. "Out here, they'll find you as much as you'll find them."

The trail wound through a kaleidoscope of textures and colors: gnarled roots curling out of the earth like ancient fingers, ferns brushing against my legs, and towering trees cloaked in emerald moss. Each step was a sensory immersion—the crunch of leaves underfoot, the soft brush of vines against my arms, and the occasional burst of color as butterflies flitted by in hues of electric blue and fiery orange.

"Congo is like that, wild and raw," Mosi said, stepping effortlessly over a fallen log. "It's untamed, yet everything here has a place, a rhythm. Even us." His words hung in the air, a reminder that we were merely guests in this ancient, intricate ecosystem.

Suddenly, Mosi stopped. His body tensed, head tilted as though catching a whisper from the forest itself. "Listen," he murmured, raising a finger for silence.

I held my breath, ears straining against the cacophony of birdsong and rustling leaves. Then, faint and deep, it came—a low, resonant rumble that seemed to reverberate through the trees. A gorilla's call. The forest seemed to close in around us, vines hanging like green curtains and the canopy above weaving a living roof. The light dimmed, creating a sense of intimacy, as though the jungle was drawing us into its secret heart.

And then, there they were.

Through a break in the foliage, I saw them—a family of gorillas nestled in a sunlit clearing. My heart leapt, a rush of awe and disbelief washing over me. A mother sat serenely, cradling her baby against her chest. Her powerful arms, capable of immense strength, held the tiny creature with infinite tenderness. Nearby, a juvenile swung playfully from a low-hanging branch, its laughter-like calls blending with the forest symphony.

"Look," Mosi whispered, motioning for me to kneel.

I sank behind a shrub, peering through its leaves like a voyeur into an extraordinary moment. The mother gorilla's eyes caught mine—deep, liquid pools of warmth and ancient wisdom. She scanned her surroundings with calm vigilance, her gaze both protective and curious. The baby, no larger than a human toddler, clung to her fur, its tiny hands gripping tightly as if seeking security in this vast, untamed world.

To the left, a young male ventured closer to us, his glossy black coat shimmering in the dappled sunlight. He moved with a mix of confidence and curiosity, plucking wildflowers from the forest floor with meticulous care. One by one, he tossed them into the air, the petals catching the light as they floated down like confetti.

"Can you believe how close we are?" Mosi murmured, his voice barely above a whisper.

I nodded, unable to tear my eyes away. The gorillas' interactions were mesmerizing—gentle touches, playful nudges, and an unspoken bond that seemed to radiate from their every movement. It was as though the world had narrowed to this single, perfect moment, leaving behind the chaos of modern life.

The mother gorilla shifted slightly, adjusting her baby as she let out a soft grunt. The juvenile, emboldened by a burst of energy, scampered toward the young male, who greeted it with a playful shove. Their laughter-like sounds filled the clearing.

Time felt suspended as I watched, each second stretching into an eternity of wonder. Here, in the heart of the forest, life unfolded in its purest form—uncomplicated, unhurried, and profoundly beautiful.

"Out here," Mosi said softly, "we're not just visitors. We're witnesses. And maybe, just maybe, protectors too."

As the family of gorillas began to move, melting back into the emerald embrace of the forest, I felt a pang of longing. This was their world—wild, raw, and breathtakingly free. And for a fleeting moment, I had been part of it. The realization was humbling, a reminder of our shared responsibility to preserve the fragile, magnificent tapestry of life that binds us all.

Refugee Camps... A Fragile Resilience

I lingered in the forest long after the gorillas had disappeared, my mind tethered to their world. The wilderness was a dreamscape, vibrant and alive, where every leaf and creature seemed to hum with purpose. Yet, the Congo's reality—its struggles, its resilience—loomed like a shadow beyond the trees.

This is a land of contradictions: unspeakable beauty set against the weight of unrelenting hardship. Even as I carried the memory of the gorillas with me, etched like a precious carving in my heart, I felt the pull of a different story. Mosi and I began our journey toward Goma, a city that teeters between hope and despair. The roads were rough, cutting through vast landscapes of volcanic rock and patches of farmland. As we entered the outskirts of the city, the air grew thicker—not with the moisture of the rainforest, but with the grit of human survival.

Goma is a place where life presses forward despite scars etched into its history. Its streets thrummed with energy: vendors hawked everything from bananas to handmade crafts, their voices rising above the din of motorbikes and laughter. There was a strange vibrancy here, a determination to claim joy even in the face of hardship.

Yet just beyond this bustle lay the refugee camps—tent cities sprawling in weary rows, temporary homes for those displaced by violence and war. The contrast hit me like a punch, stark and unrelenting.

We approached the camp, and the landscape shifted into one of stark reality. Thin, tattered tents flapped in the wind, their patched plastic walls barely holding back the elements. Muddy paths wound between shelters, where children with wide, curious eyes played with scraps of discarded plastic and makeshift toys. A woman emerged from one of the tents, her frame slender but unbowed. She held a child close, their faces framed by shadows and streaked with resilience. "We hope to return home," she said, her voice a soft breeze against the weight of her reality.

Her words lingered, hanging in the air like a prayer whispered to an indifferent sky. What struck me most was not the despair but her strength. In her tired smile, I saw something almost luminous—a flicker of hope that refused to be extinguished.

"Every visit matters," Mosi said as we walked back. "When you listen, when you see, you carry their stories with you. And stories can change the world."

The Congo does not offer easy answers. It demands that you sit with its complexities, that you feel its pain and marvel at its beauty in equal measure. The rainforest had shown me life at its most primal and unspoiled, and now Goma revealed the fragility of human existence—and the courage that rises from it.

This journey was no longer about me. It wasn't about the photographs I'd taken or the moments I'd captured. It was about the lives I'd glimpsed, the stories that had reached across the vast chasm of our differences to find a home in my heart. As we drove away, I turned to look back at the camp one last time. The tents shimmered in the afternoon heat. And in their midst, I saw something extraordinary: life continuing, children laughing, mothers comforting, people dreaming of a better tomorrow. If you ever find yourself in this land—this enigmatic, heartbreaking, breathtaking Congo—remember that it is a place that will challenge you in ways you cannot predict.

Secure your visa, yes. Pack your essentials, certainly. But more than that, pack your capacity to listen. Bring your willingness to be vulnerable, to learn, to let this land and its people change you. Travel is not always a search for the spectacular; sometimes, it is a pilgrimage into the raw, unfiltered essence of what it means to be human. And in the Congo, that essence will meet you at every turn—in the laughter of children, the courage of a mother, the wisdom of a guide, and the wild, indomitable spirit of the land itself.

When you leave, you will not leave unchanged. And that is the greatest gift this journey can offer.

Chapter VII

MADAGASCAR

April 2023

> ***The wild woman is only intimidating to those who are not yet free.***
>
> **– *Shikoba Wolfe***

There are two kinds of travelers who plan a trip to Madagascar. The first group can't help but think of the animated DreamWorks movie, where animals break into dance and the island's charm is painted in bright, whimsical colors. The second group—ours—hears the voice of David Attenborough narrating the untamed wilderness: a place where nature runs wild, unedited, and the soundtrack is the chorus of rainforests rather than pop tunes.

As the plane descended over the Indian Ocean, Madagascar loomed below us like a giant, sun-soaked emerald. I pressed my forehead against the window, marveling at the contrast between its jagged coastlines and the dense tapestry of green that stretched as far as I could see. *This wasn't just another stop on my journey—it was the one I'd been waiting for.* I turned to my husband, who wore an expression I knew all too well: a mix of excitement and disbelief. It was the look of someone standing on the edge of a long-held dream.

"Can you believe we're finally here?" I said, my voice barely a whisper.

He nodded, eyes wide, taking in the scene as if he were imprinting it into his memory. The air felt different the moment we stepped off the plane—humid, fragrant, and alive with a hundred different sounds. Cicadas buzzed, lemurs called out in the distance, and the earthy scent of wet foliage filled our lungs.

Madagascar is a place that resists simple definitions. Separated from the African mainland over 80 million years ago, it has evolved in isolation, a lost world where 90% of the species are found nowhere else on Earth. For me, it felt like stepping into the pages of *The Jungle Book*, which as I have mentioned earlier in the book, is a story I had clung to as a child, imagining myself as Mowgli—barefoot, free, and at home in the wild. This love for the untamed world had shaped so much of my life, driving me to places where others feared to tread, and here, in Madagascar, it felt like I was finally living that childhood fantasy.

Our local guide, Tiana, met us with a warm smile and a twinkle in his eye. "Welcome to Madagascar," he said, shaking our hands. "This trip isn't just about seeing exotic animals, you know. It's about entering their world and understanding what it takes for them to survive here."

He led us along the red dirt roads that wound through landscapes unlike anything we had ever seen. Towering baobabs lined the horizon like ancient sentinels, their thick, bulbous trunks reaching skyward as if defying gravity itself. These iconic trees, some over a thousand years old, are known as the 'upside-down trees' because their bare branches look like roots suspended in the air. Villagers moved through the scene, balancing baskets on their heads, their faces lit with smiles as they waved to us.

"Did you know that baobabs can store up to 30,000 liters of water in their trunks?" Tiana said, catching our curious glances. "It's how they survive the long dry seasons. They're like the island's silent, stoic guardians."

I felt a rush of appreciation for this land—a place where adaptation is a way of life. Even after visiting more than 30 countries across Africa, Madagascar was unlike anything I had experienced before. It was a biological melting pot, and every inch of it seemed to be bursting with life. We hiked through jungles so dense the light barely filtered through the canopy. The forest floor was a mosaic of ferns, mosses, and fungi, each step sinking into a thick, damp carpet that seemed to pulse with hidden life.

"Look up!" my husband called, breaking my reverie. He pointed at a flash of movement among the branches. There they were—our first lemurs. A troop of ring-tailed lemurs, their long black-and-white tails trailing behind them like streamers, leaped gracefully from branch to branch. They paused to study us, their wide eyes brimming with a curiosity that mirrored our own.

"They're watching us as much as we're watching them," I laughed, unable to tear my gaze away.

"They're sacred here," Tiana said. "In Malagasy culture, some believe lemurs are the souls of our ancestors, keeping an eye on the living."

I couldn't help but smile. It reminded me of the stories I had grown up with—the idea that the jungle was a living, breathing entity, filled with characters that spoke in whispers and glances. As a child, I had memorized passages from *The Jungle Book*, convinced that if I listened hard enough, the wild would reveal its secrets to me. Here in Madagascar, it felt as though the forest was doing just that.

We moved deeper into the forest, and I felt like I was stepping into a scene from a nature documentary. Everywhere I looked, there were animals blending into their surroundings like nature's own camouflage artists. A brilliantly colored panther chameleon clung to a branch, its skin shifting from green to yellow and then to a dazzling blue. It felt like witnessing a living canvas, painted and repainted in real time.

"Chameleons are the true masters of disguise," Tiana whispered. "Did you know Madagascar has about half of the world's chameleon species? Some of them are so tiny, they could sit comfortably on your fingertip," he continued.

We crouched down to admire the intricate patterns of a leaf-tailed gecko, its body so perfectly mimicking the decaying leaves around it that I wouldn't have noticed it if Tiana hadn't pointed it out. Frogs, each more vibrantly colored than the last, sat still as stones, their bright hues warning of toxins potent enough to deter any predator.

"There's a reason why this island is called the 'eighth continent,'" Tiana mused. "The biodiversity here is unrivaled. It's a world within a world." We arrived at our lodge, a simple yet charming place nestled among the trees, with vibrant flowers blooming all around. I breathed in deeply, savoring the mingling scents of fresh rain and wild blossoms. We settled onto our porch, looking out over a dense forest that seemed to stretch endlessly.

"This place feels like magic," my husband whispered in awe.

I nodded, my heart swelling with the same feeling. "It's more than that," I replied. "It's like finding a piece of your soul you didn't know was missing. It's the call of the wild I've felt since I was a little girl, dreaming of faraway jungles."

The sun began its descent, casting a golden glow over the landscape. As we watched, the forest seemed to come alive with the calls of nocturnal creatures waking from their slumber. The rhythm of Madagascar was unlike anything I had felt before—raw, wild, and unyielding, yet serene and timeless.

"Let's dive into the wild," I said with a grin, turning to my husband. "I want to understand what makes this place so special." And with that, we set off into the unknown, ready to uncover the secrets of a land where nature reigns supreme and adventure waits around every corner.

Morondava... *Avenue of the Baobabs*

The Avenue of the Baobabs in Morondava was a scene straight out of a dream. I'd seen photos of these trees before—those fantastical, towering giants that seemed to defy both time and gravity. In every picture, the baobabs looked like something out of a dream, their thick, bulbous trunks reaching skyward like ancient, upside-down roots. But as we approached this iconic landscape in person, I realized no photograph could ever capture the pure, palpable presence of these trees.

The road was little more than a sandy, ochre path flanked by the looming silhouettes of baobabs, their bare branches stretching up like skeletal fingers against the sky. It felt as though we had stumbled upon a hidden portal to another world, a place where time moved differently—if it moved at all. I glanced at my husband, whose eyes mirrored my own sense of wonder.

"Look at those!" I exclaimed, pointing at a cluster of the tallest baobabs, their swollen trunks thick with the stories of centuries. Each one was a living relic, older than many empires, and they stood like guardians of a forgotten era, whispering secrets of the earth into the wind.

"They look like they've been plucked out of a fairytale," he murmured.

We parked the jeep and stepped into the warm, fragrant air, heavy with the scent of dry earth and distant rain. The baobabs here aren't just trees; they are ancestral beings. Locals call them 'Renala,' or 'Mother of the Forest,' for good reason. Some of these giants are believed to be over 1,000 years old, standing tall as silent witnesses to the rise and fall of civilizations, the ebb and flow of nature's grand design.

As we walked, I couldn't help but recall a passage from *The Jungle Book*. I remembered Mowgli's awe as he looked up at the towering trees of the jungle, and I felt a flicker of that same childlike wonder ignite within me now. Here I was, standing in a place that felt every bit as mythical as the pages of Kipling's tale.

"You know why they call these trees 'upside-down' trees, right?" our local guide, Marcel, asked with a grin. He had a knack for storytelling, and I could see the delight in his eyes as he shared his knowledge.

"Because their branches look like roots?" my husband guessed.

Marcel nodded. "Yes, exactly. During the dry season, they shed their leaves, and it's said they reach for the sky as if they've been uprooted and replanted upside down by the gods."

The sun began to dip lower, casting long shadows that stretched across the reddish-brown earth. We found ourselves surrounded by a golden glow, the kind that makes you feel like the world has slowed just for a moment, inviting you to pause and simply breathe it all in. The sky ignited in shades of orange, pink, and violet, and I felt a sense of stillness, a rare quiet that settled over us like a soft blanket.

“We have to come back at sunrise,” I said, almost breathless from the beauty of it all. And so we did—three times, in fact. Each visit was like seeing the world anew. The dawn light brought with it a delicate touch, soft pastels washing over the baobabs, casting them as gentle giants against a sky that was just beginning to wake. The trees stood like pillars of an ancient temple, shrouded in morning mist, their shadows long and serene on the dew-kissed earth. Birds began their morning calls, a symphony of life awakening, and we stood in reverence, feeling as though we were intruding on a sacred ritual.

The locals believe that these trees hold the spirits of their ancestors, and it wasn’t hard to see why. At sunset, the baobabs transformed once more, silhouettes etched against a fiery sky. We sat quietly, watching as the day gave way to night, the Milky Way unfurling overhead in a dazzling display of stars. It was a sky unlike any I had seen before, the kind that makes you feel the vastness of the universe and the smallness of your own existence.

“What do you prefer—sunrise or sunset?” my husband asked, breaking the comfortable silence between us.

I smiled, shaking my head. “I can’t choose. It’s like trying to pick a favorite heartbeat.”

Our final visit came at nightfall, under a sky draped in stardust. The air was cool, the village fires crackled softly in the distance, and the smell of wood smoke mingled with the sweet scent of tamarind. Marcel had built a small fire, and we sat around it with a few villagers who shared stories in Malagasy in their gentle voices.

"Legend says that the first baobab was planted by a mischievous spirit," Marcel said, his face lit by the glow of the fire. "But the tree grew so tall and proud that the spirit became angry and yanked it out of the ground, planting it back upside down to teach it humility." I laughed at the thought, imagining these ancient giants with their roots exposed to the heavens. In a place like this, it wasn't hard to believe in legends. It felt as though the trees themselves were listening, their gnarled branches swaying softly in agreement.

On our last evening, I lingered behind as the others walked back to the jeep. I pressed my hand against the rough bark of one of the oldest baobabs, feeling its texture, coarse and timeworn. It was a silent exchange—a moment of connection across centuries. I closed my eyes, letting the wind carry the whispers of the forest. This wasn't just a journey across landscapes; it was a journey inward. Here in Madagascar, among the baobabs that have outlived kings and empires, I felt a reminder of something I had always known but sometimes forgot in the rush of everyday life: The wild places of the world don't just call us to explore; they call us to remember who we are.

In the presence of these ancient trees, I felt both small and infinitely vast, a fleeting moment in the grand timeline of the universe. And yet, as we drove away, the words from *The Jungle Book* danced in my mind once more: *The strength of the pack is the wolf, and the strength of the wolf is the pack.* I realized then that this place, these trees, this earth beneath my feet—it was all a part of my pack, and I, theirs.

Kirindy National Park

With the Avenue of Baobabs still lingering in my mind like the memory of a dream, we set our sights on Kirindy National Park—a landscape that promised to reveal Madagascar's wild soul. Kirindy was no ordinary forest. It's the kind of place that hums with life, where the air thrums with secrets of creatures unseen by most, a living labyrinth dense with possibility. As our jeep rattled along the rugged, red-dirt road, a cloud of fine dust billowed behind us, catching the sun's dying light like a plume of golden smoke. I glanced over at my husband, his fingers absently adjusting his camera strap, his eyes alight with the same thrill I felt buzzing through me.

"Kirindy is home to the fossa, you know," I said aloud, unable to hide my excitement. He grinned, the kind of grin that has a shared history behind it. "And the dancing sifakas," he added, raising his eyebrows in mock anticipation. "I'm ready for their acrobatics."

The park greeted us with a blend of earthy musk and floral sweetness, the scent of damp soil mingled with the heady perfume of unseen blossoms. Towering trees formed a cathedral-like canopy overhead, their leaves dappling the forest floor in soft shadows. We stepped out into this green embrace, a world away from everything familiar. A hush fell as we began our hike along the narrow, winding trail. The symphony of the forest wrapped around us—chirps, rustles, and the distant call of a bird echoing through the treetops. I stopped in my tracks, motioning for silence, and there, suspended mid-air, was the first of many wonders: a family of white sifakas. These lemurs, with their creamy coats and golden eyes, seemed almost ethereal in the waning light. They moved with a fluid grace, leaping between branches as if propelled by invisible wings.

"There they are," I whispered, unable to hide my awe.

My husband's camera clicked rapidly, capturing their mid-air pirouettes. He glanced at me, his face flushed with exhilaration. "They're like forest ballerinas," he said, lowering his lens for a moment just to watch, unmediated by technology.

I nodded, struck by how they seemed to dance not just with each other but with the very essence of the forest around them. It was as though their joy was contagious, seeping into our bones, making us feel lighter, more connected to this untamed place.

The dusk descended into night, and we prepared for one of Kirindy's most anticipated experiences—a nocturnal walk, where the forest transforms into a world of shadow and silhouette, revealing a different cast of characters. We equipped ourselves with flashlights, their beams piercing the thick darkness like spears of moonlight.

"Stay close," my husband murmured, the playful confidence of the day replaced by a reverent whisper. The forest at night demanded a certain humility; it was no longer our playground but a realm we were merely allowed to tiptoe into. The air cooled, thick with the scent of leaves and the lingering heat of the day. We crept through the underbrush, senses heightened, straining to catch every rustle, every fleeting glimpse of life. Then, in the soft glow of our lights, a pair of wide, reflective eyes stared back at us—tiny, round, and almost comical. A mouse lemur, the smallest primate in the world, clung to a low branch, its delicate fingers gripping the bark. It blinked at us, as if weighing whether we were friend or foe, before scampering into the shadows.

"Did you see that?" I said in a low voice, the sheer joy of it bubbling up in laughter.

"Yes," he whispered back, grinning. "It's like a miniature gremlin." We moved deeper into the forest, listening as the calls of nocturnal birds layered over the steady drone of crickets—a wild orchestra performed under a sky speckled with stars. Somewhere above, the sound of a lemur's eerie mating call echoed, a note of longing that cut through the symphony.

"Do you hear that?" I asked, transfixed. "It's like the forest itself is singing."

He nodded, his face upturned toward the canopy, eyes searching for the invisible creature that had called out.

"They're announcing themselves," he said softly. "Letting the forest know they're here."

We pressed on, feeling the forest close in around us, its stories whispering from every corner. The air pulsed with life; it was as if the very ground beneath our feet was a living entity, vibrating with energy. The deeper we ventured, the more we realized how little we knew about this place.

The trail eventually opened into a clearing, bathed in the silver light of the moon. We paused there, catching our breath, listening to the far-off rustle of leaves, the soft call of an owl. In that moment, it struck me just how immense the world was, how full of surprises it could still be, even for seasoned travelers like us.

"What do you think?" I asked, turning to my husband. He lowered his flashlight, meeting my gaze with a smile that was softer now, more contemplative. "I think we're lucky," he said simply. "To be here, to witness this."

I nodded, feeling a swell of gratitude rise in my chest. Here, in the heart of Kirindy, surrounded by creatures that seemed plucked from a storybook, it was impossible not to be humbled. We were visitors, temporary guests in a world that would go on without us, wild and beautiful, untamed and eternal. And as we made our way back, the forest slowly retreating into silence, I knew that this night would linger with us long after we left Madagascar. A memory carved deep into the fabric of our lives—a reminder of the world's untamed magic and the joy of discovering it together.

Tsingy National Park

Getting to Tsingy National Park isn't just a journey—it's an initiation. Here's what I mean – it took us three days of relentless travel, every bone-jarring jolt on dirt roads, every precarious river crossing testing not just the limits of endurance but also of our sense of humor, to finally get there. By the end of it, you're stripped of any lingering romantic notions about the 'road less traveled.' This wasn't a road; it was a test of mettle.

It all started at the ungodly hour of 5 a.m., the kind of morning where the sky is still the color of charcoal. I was dragged from sleep by that giddy cocktail of excitement and the sharp realization that we might have underestimated what lay ahead.

"Ready for this?" I asked my husband as we hoisted ourselves onto a bullock cart, its wooden frame groaning under our weight. He shot me a wry smile, rubbing the sleep from his eyes. "Do I have a choice?"

The cart lurched forward, the oxen's hooves clopping rhythmically against the hard-packed dirt. We swayed with each bump, our laughter mingling with the early morning sounds of the waking village. It was absurd, this form of travel—a throwback to another century. I felt like a time traveler, slipping into an era when patience was the price of adventure.

After an hour of bone-rattling jolts, we disembarked to board not one but *two* ferries—if you could call them that.

These weren't the sleek vessels of postcard scenes; they were haphazard contraptions, barely staying afloat on the muddy, swollen river. The waters reflected the sky's gradual shift from black to a soft, pre-dawn blue. We leaned over the edge, watching the current swirl, wondering if we'd reach the other side before the boats decided to give up the ghost.

"Think this thing's going to hold?" I asked, eyeing a suspicious crack near the bow. He shrugged, snapping photos of the mist lifting off the water. "We'll find out, won't we?" Seventeen grueling hours later, long after the sun had dipped behind the horizon and our patience had worn thin, we staggered into our hotel. It was past 1 a.m. by then, and exhaustion had settled into our bones like a deep ache. Still, there was an undercurrent of anticipation humming beneath the weariness, like a promise half-whispered in the dark. But the fatigue was punctuated by a moment that stayed with me long after the journey. It was a fleeting stop in a tiny village, where a swarm of children appeared seemingly out of nowhere. Their faces were lit up with unfiltered joy. We sat down, sharing what little food we had left—crackers, dried fruit, whatever was in our pockets. I pulled out a frisbee, something I'd packed on a whim, and tossed it toward the group. It took a moment, but then one child leapt up, catching it with an unpracticed grace. The air filled with shrieks of laughter as they took turns, the bright disc slicing through the air like a sliver of sunlight.

"Look at them," I whispered, my throat tight with emotion. "This is pure joy." My husband, watching with a soft smile, nodded. "You can't buy that kind of happiness."

Standing at the gates of Tsingy National Park the next morning felt surreal, as if we'd been transported to an alien world. The landscape stretched out before us in a jagged, spiky expanse—limestone pinnacles rising like the serrated teeth of a monster, remnants of an ancient ocean floor. It was impossible not to feel small here, dwarfed by these sharp sentinels forged by time and tide. "This place is insane," my husband muttered, staring up at the towering spikes that clawed at the sky.

"Not for the faint-hearted," I replied, tightening the straps on my backpack. "Or the faint-footed."

We plunged into the labyrinth, the path winding like a ribbon through this otherworldly maze. Within minutes, we were scrambling over razor-sharp rocks, their edges threatening to slice through our resolve. Giant spiderwebs, thick as silk tapestries, hung like veils between the stone spires, swaying gently in the breeze. At one point, I nearly walked face-first into a wasp nest, its inhabitants buzzing angrily as if warning me to watch where I was going.

"You okay?" he asked, pulling me back just in time.

"Close call," I laughed, my heart pounding. "But this is incredible, isn't it?"

We pressed on, clambering over rocks that felt as though they'd crumble beneath our weight, ducking into narrow crevices where the world narrowed into darkness. It was a place that demanded respect—every step a negotiation with nature, every climb a leap of faith. The deeper we went, the more the sounds of the forest seemed to recede, replaced by the echo of our breaths, the scrape of our boots against ancient stone.

Hours later, we emerged at a summit, the view unfurling before us like a painting coming to life. The forest stretched out below, a sea of emerald-green canopies interrupted by the spiky silhouettes of the Tsingy. It looked like the back of a stegosaurus, undulating across the horizon. I stood there, gulping in the cool air, feeling a rush of euphoria and something else—something like reverence.

"Worth it?" I asked, turning to my husband. He didn't respond immediately, just wrapped an arm around my shoulders, pulling me close. We stood there, silent witnesses to a vista that felt almost holy in its untouched beauty. "More than worth it," he finally said. "This is why we travel, isn't it?" I nodded, unable to find the words. In that moment, all the hours of discomfort, the fatigue, the uncertainty—they melted away. We were left with only this: the feeling of being small in a big, wild world, and the thrill of having found our way to a corner of it that so few get to see.

Andasibe

Mitsinjo National Park, Andasibe National Park, Vakona Private Reserve

The next chapter of our Madagascar journey led us into the heart of Andasibe, a lush rainforest that felt like a living, breathing entity. Mitsinjo and Andasibe National Parks, along with the Vakona Private Reserve, unfolded before us like a vibrant tapestry of sound and color. The air buzzed with the hum of cicadas and the rustling of leaves. I felt as if we had stepped into another realm—a sanctuary where nature's symphony played on an endless loop.

Our mission was clear: find lemurs. Madagascar is home to more than a hundred unique species, and the excitement of spotting these incredible creatures fueled our every step. "I can't wait to see an Indri," I confessed, eyes scanning the emerald canopy above. The Indri, the largest living lemur, is famous for its eerie, whale-like calls that resonate through the forest like ancient songs carried by the wind. Hours passed in a dreamlike blur as we trekked deeper into the forest, guided by the distant echo of Indri's call. It was a sound both haunting and beautiful, like a cry from a prehistoric world. "Did you hear that?" I asked, my voice tinged with awe.

"Yes, it's close," my husband replied, his own excitement mirroring mine. "Let's follow it."

We navigated through the dense undergrowth, the forest floor springy beneath our feet. Then, there it was—a pair of Indris perched high in the treetops. Their black-and-white fur seemed to glow against the vibrant greens of the foliage. One turned its head, locking eyes with me for a brief, spellbinding moment. It was as if the forest itself had paused, allowing us a glimpse into its ancient secrets.

As we ventured on, we stumbled upon a troupe of Golden Sifakas. Their golden fur gleamed in the dappled sunlight as they leapt gracefully from branch to branch. Watching them felt like witnessing a choreographed dance, each leap and swing a part of an exquisite, silent ballet. I couldn't help but laugh at their playful movements, their sideways hops across branches like nature's acrobats performing just for us.

And then, another discovery—the elusive Black-and-White Ruffed Lemur, its striking coat blending into the thick vines as it nibbled on ripe fruit. I felt a swell of gratitude, a sense of privilege at being so close to these gentle creatures. The moment felt delicate, a reminder of how fragile this ecosystem truly is. "Imagine a world without them," I said, almost to myself. "It's heartbreaking." My husband squeezed my hand in quiet agreement. "That's why we're here," he said softly. "We can't just look away."

We made our way to a section of the forest teeming with reptiles, including Madagascar's famed chameleons. The sheer diversity was astounding—over 150 species found only here, on this island that seems to defy the laws of evolution. We marveled at a Weiled Chameleon, its ridged head and telescopic eyes darting about as it seamlessly changed color to blend with the bark of a nearby tree. It shifted from bright emerald green to a muted brown, a transformation so fluid it felt like watching an artist's brushstrokes come to life.

Next, we encountered the Parson's Chameleon, a giant among its kind, with scales that shimmered in shades of turquoise and gold. It crept slowly, almost regally, across a sunlit branch; its body was like a masterpiece of color and texture. I watched in awe, unable to tear my eyes away. Then there was the tiny Mantella frog, its vivid carrot-orange skin popping against the damp, dark earth—a splash of color in the forest's muted palette.

"Look at that!" I exclaimed, crouching low to get a better look. "It's like finding a gem in the undergrowth."

I could feel my inner David Attenborough bubbling with joy, but beneath the excitement lay a growing sense of urgency. Madagascar holds a staggering 5% of the world's plant and animal species, yet the survival of these incredible creatures is threatened by deforestation, climate change, and illegal poaching. Our visit culminated at a local reforestation center run by an inspiring NGO, dedicated to preserving the fragile ecosystem. We spent the afternoon planting young saplings—tiny promises of a future forest, our hands sinking into the cool, dark soil. The physical act of digging, planting, and patting down the earth felt grounding, a small but tangible contribution to the larger fight for conservation.

"This isn't just a holiday," I said, wiping the sweat from my brow as I looked around at the rows of newly planted trees. "It's a call to action."

He nodded, a look of quiet determination on his face. "We can't just be passive observers anymore. This is personal now."

As we made our way back through the forest. The air filled once again with the chorus of the forest—a final serenade to end the day. I took one last, lingering look around, feeling the weight of the experience settle into my bones. Andasibe had given us more than just unforgettable encounters with wildlife; it had given us a new sense of responsibility.

"We'll come back," I said, almost as a promise to the forest, the lemurs, the chameleons, and the Mantella frogs.

"Yes," my husband replied, slinging his camera over his shoulder. "We'll come back, and next time, we'll bring more people with us."

Andasibe is the heartbeat of Madagascar, a wild, untamed reminder of what the world stands to lose if we don't act. This was more than just travel; it was advocacy, wrapped in adventure, and a journey that had transformed us as much as the landscape itself.

The Call of Madagascar

From the towering baobabs to the playful lemurs, from the jagged peaks to the sweeping rainforests, Madagascar is a wild, beating heart of untamed nature and ancient rhythms.

I found myself overwhelmed here, not just by the sheer beauty of the landscape but by the sense of connection, of stepping into a world that has existed long before us and will, hopefully, endure long after. There is a magic in knowing that over 95% of Madagascar's flora and fauna cannot be found anywhere else on Earth—a fact that both astonishes and humbles. I felt a deep responsibility with every footfall on its ancient trails, a desire to leave nothing behind but a soft footprint, to be part of the conservation efforts that strive to keep this place as it is, wild and unspoiled.

But this isn't the kind of journey you can plan down to the last detail. You have to surrender a part of yourself here.

Let go of the tightly packed itineraries, the need for constant connectivity, the urge to tick off a list of sights like some kind of collector. This is a place where you might find more joy in the moments between the grand experiences. I remember sitting quietly on the forest floor, listening to the rustle of leaves as a chameleon crept by. In that moment, it was just me and this tiny, otherworldly creature, sharing a brief sliver of time together. It was pure, unfiltered awe.

Madagascar is the kind of adventure that shifts your soul's compass, recalibrates the way you see the world. It's not just about the thrill of seeing a rare lemur or snorkeling in waters so clear you can see a whole ecosystem thriving beneath you. It's about feeling your heart beat in time with the pulse of the land. It's about understanding that travel isn't just about seeing—it's about being seen by the world, allowing yourself to be changed by it in ways you never expected. We made it a point to travel thoughtfully here, engaging with local guides who shared their stories, their hopes, and their fears for the future of this island. We spent hours in local markets, tasting dishes that defied description, woven together with spices, histories, and the warmth of a welcoming smile. We weren't just passing through; we were living it, and in doing so, we became part of the tapestry of this place, however briefly.

So if you're seeking adventure, if you're craving something different—choose Madagascar. But don't come here expecting the familiar. Come for the unknown. Come ready to be uncomfortable, to step off the beaten path, to discover not just what lies in the depths of the rainforests or the clear blue waters, but what lies within you when you're far from everything you know.

Let the lemurs lead you to places you hadn't thought to look. Listen to the whispers of the baobabs as they tell you stories written in their rings. And when you find yourself, as I did, standing beneath the canopy of Andasibe, surrounded by the symphony of the forest at dusk—let yourself be still. Let yourself feel the weight of the moment, the fleeting, fragile beauty of this island that refuses to fit neatly into any box.

Because once you've experienced the raw, untamed spirit of Madagascar, you'll carry it with you, like a seed planted deep in your heart. It will call to you when you least expect it, a soft, insistent whisper: come back. Come back, not just to see more, but to see it differently, to sink deeper into its wild embrace. And I know I will.

Chapter VIII

GABON

June 2024

> ***And into the forest I go, to lose my mind and find my soul.***
>
> ***– John Muir***

The anticipation fizzled inside me, bubbling up like the spray of the Atlantic crashing against Gabon's rugged coastline. Known as *Africa's Last Eden,* this wild sanctuary had been calling to me with a quiet urgency. Gabon is a place where the pulse of the natural world beats louder than the noise of human progress, where you can almost feel the earth breathe beneath your feet. For weeks, I had meticulously planned this journey, but no amount of preparation could compare to the thrill of actually being here—on the brink of stepping into a land that feels like it's still cradled in the hands of time.

"Ready for some real wildlife?" my husband grinned, eyes sparkling with the kind of excitement that only an untamed adventure can bring. His question felt almost rhetorical—we both knew this was the moment we'd been waiting for. It wasn't just a trip; it was a pilgrimage to one of the last strongholds of raw, unblemished wilderness on the continent.

Our journey was nothing short of epic. We hopped across continents on a series of flights, then switched to boats that navigated winding waterways, each transfer pulling us deeper into the heart of the wild. The rhythm of travel became a kind of initiation; with every bumpy ride and delayed connection, we shed layers of city life and slipped further into the embrace of the forest. By the time we boarded our final boat, the humid breeze tousling my hair, I felt as if we were being welcomed into a sacred, hidden world. The dense foliage seemed to bow over us like a green cathedral ceiling, whispering secrets from centuries ago.

Set on the equator, Gabon straddles a vibrant line between land and sea. It's a country that cradles ancient lowland rainforests, savannahs, and mangroves within its borders. Here, wildlife reigns supreme: lowland gorillas forage among the underbrush, chimpanzees swing through towering canopy trees, and humpback whales breach in the Atlantic waters offshore. It's a biodiversity hotspot, holding within its borders one of the richest collections of plant and animal life in the world. But this abundance comes at a cost—tourism here isn't for the faint of heart or the hurried traveler. This is a place for those willing to earn their experience, to put in the work required to explore a landscape that remains untamed and, for the most part, uncharted.

On paper, Gabon has it all. But reality paints a more complex picture. Unlike the well-trodden paths of the Serengeti or the bustling lodges of Kruger, Gabon's trails are elusive, its lodges sparse. It takes patience and persistence to plan a safari here. You can't just book a flight and expect to step into luxury accommodations; you need to navigate permits, sketchy transportation links, and a landscape that can be as unforgiving as it is breathtaking. Yet, this is exactly what reassures me—the more challenging the expedition, the more it promises an authentic connection to the wild. It's the kind of place where you can still hear the sound of your own footsteps over the call of the forest, where the sky belongs more to birds of prey than to charter planes.

We finally arrived at our lodge nestled deep within Loango National Park, a place that felt as though it was perched on the edge of the world. The park is often dubbed *the Land of the Surfing Hippos,* a nickname born from the rare sight of hippos wading into the ocean's waves. As we disembarked, the smell of salt and moss filled the air, and I caught my first glimpse of a dense, impenetrable forest stretching endlessly toward the horizon. Here, the land meets the sea in a stunning fusion, where elephants wander onto beaches and buffalo tracks crisscross tidal flats.

Our guide, a wiry woman with a sun-etched face and the easy grace of someone who knows this land intimately, greeted us with a wide smile. "Welcome to Gabon," she said. "Here, the forest teaches patience and respect. You cannot rush the wild." Her words lingered, and I felt a surge of gratitude—

both for being here and for being guided by someone who understood this place in a way only a local could.

Gabon isn't the safari experience most people imagine; it's not about ticking off the Big Five. It's about immersing yourself in the slow, ancient rhythms of the natural world. This is where you come to witness the quiet drama of a silverback gorilla leading his family through the undergrowth or the awe-inspiring sight of leatherback turtles heaving themselves ashore to lay eggs under a moonlit sky.

The Loango National Park

The journey to Loango National Park felt like a passage into a forgotten world—a realm where nature rules unchallenged and time seems to linger in reverence. We boarded a small plane from Libreville, its engines roaring as we ascended over a patchwork of dense rainforest and shimmering lagoons. The quick stop in Port Gentil was a fleeting glimpse of urban life before we plunged deeper into Gabon's wilderness. My heart raced with anticipation as we left behind the familiar hum of city streets and ventured toward the unknown.

The four-hour drive that followed was a bone-rattling odyssey through thick jungle, the road more a suggestion than a reality. The tires bounced over rough terrain; each jolt was a reminder that the best adventures are never smooth. I stared out at the emerald curtain of trees enveloping us, imagining the creatures that lived unseen beneath their shadowed canopy—gorillas foraging, elephants carving paths through the underbrush, and the faint rustle of a leopard on the prowl.

Finally, we reached the port. I smiled at the sight of our boat, bobbing in the gentle swell of the estuary. The hour-long ride through the mangroves felt like drifting into a living painting: tangled roots dipped into the water like ancient fingers, while sunlight dappled the rippling surface in shades of gold and green. It was as if the landscape itself had choreographed this serene spectacle just for us, a secret performance of nature's raw elegance.

As we approached the lodge, nestled on the shores of the Louri Lagoon, I could barely contain my awe. It was both humble and majestic—a cluster of tented cabins that seemed to rise organically from the forest floor. The lodge's design, with its canvas walls and wooden furnishings, whispered of a deep respect for the surrounding wilderness, blending seamlessly into the environment as if it had always been there.

"This is incredible," I murmured, taking in the earthy tones and simple yet elegant decor. The sea breeze carried the scent of salt and wood, wrapping around me like a welcoming embrace. Each morning began with a symphony of birdsong that seemed to rise with the sun. As I sipped my coffee on the deck, the air thick with the scent of damp earth, I watched egrets glide effortlessly across the lagoon, their white wings cutting through the mist like brushstrokes on a canvas.

Our days were filled with exploration—safaris into the heart of Loango's dense forest, or boat rides through the vast lagoon teeming with life. Our guide, a local conservationist named Biyela, spoke passionately about the importance of Gabon's preservation efforts. "This land belongs to the animals as much as it belongs to us," she said, her voice carrying the weight of someone who has dedicated her life to this cause. "We're merely guests here."

Loango is often called the *Land of the Surfing Hippos,* a nickname born from the rare sight of hippos venturing into the ocean waves. The park's diverse habitats, from mangroves and savannahs to untouched beaches, create a mosaic of ecosystems unlike anywhere else in Africa. As we ventured deeper, the wild world opened up before us—a baby crocodile basking on a sunlit log, its tiny body an echo of prehistoric times, or the flicker of a monitor lizard disappearing into the undergrowth.

In the evenings, we gathered around a crackling fire on the beach. The sky blazed with hues of orange and purple, a kaleidoscope of colors that painted everything in soft, dreamlike tones. Waves lapped gently at the shore, and their rhythmic song lulled us into a peaceful silence. It was a moment suspended in time, untouched by the frenzy of modern life.

At night, as I lay in our tent, the sounds of the forest enveloped me—distant calls of nocturnal creatures and the gentle whisper of the ocean. Sleep came easily, my dreams filled with visions of the wilderness and the untold stories it held.

Local Culture and the Role of Ecotourism

Beyond its natural beauty, Gabon's culture is as rich and diverse as its landscape. The people of Gabon, predominantly from the Bantu ethnic group, have deep-rooted traditions connected to the land. The Fang people, known for their intricate wood carvings and masks, believe that the forest is a spiritual place, inhabited by ancestors and spirits that guide their lives. We were told of ceremonies where villagers gather to sing and dance, invoking the spirits for guidance and protection.

Ecotourism has become a crucial tool for both preserving Gabon's environment and supporting local communities. By focusing on sustainable practices, Gabon has managed to attract a niche group of travelers who seek immersive and responsible travel experiences rather than mass tourism. This shift has created jobs, funded conservation projects, and fostered a sense of pride among locals who now see the value in protecting their natural heritage.

Gabon had opened my eyes to the delicate dance between humanity and nature, showing me that true adventure lies not just in seeking new places but in understanding and respecting them. It was a reminder that there are still corners of the world where the wild things thrive, where you can step lightly and leave only footprints behind.

This journey had not only expanded my view of ecotourism but had also connected me more deeply with the rhythms of the earth. I left Gabon with a renewed sense of purpose and a promise to return—because in places like this, the adventure never truly ends.

Reflections on Gabon

"Was it worth it?" I asked myself, leaning back against the rough-hewn chair as I soaked in the view of the lagoon—a shimmering expanse that seemed to hold the entire sky's reflection. In this corner of Africa, where the wilderness breathes freely and undisturbed, I found a slice of the world that felt as though it had escaped time's relentless march forward.

Gabon had pulled me into its embrace like no other place. Here, each day felt like an unpolished gem, filled with moments that demanded attention. This wasn't your typical safari, with manicured paths and guaranteed sightings. Instead, it was raw, unpredictable, and beautifully untamed. The country's isolation and low population density had preserved an ecosystem that thrived in the absence of human footprints, a testament to nature's resilience when given room to flourish.

I turned to my husband, who was busy scanning the dense foliage with binoculars. "This place makes me feel like we've stepped off the map," I mused, watching the awe on his face mirror my own. Planning the journey had been a puzzle of logistical challenges, but that only added to the excitement. Gabon doesn't offer itself up easily; it must be earned, every encounter a reward for those who venture beyond the well-worn trails of African tourism. "Nothing here is guaranteed," I remarked one evening as we sat by the campfire, watching the sky melt into a canvas of purples and golds. "And that's what makes it unforgettable."

We trailed herds of forest elephants through silent mangroves, caught glimpses of red river hogs slipping through the dense underbrush, and watched hippos laze in lagoons under the midday sun. Each encounter wasn't just a sighting; it was a moment of communion, a reminder of the fragile balance we were privileged to witness.

Ecotourism in Gabon goes beyond mere observation—it's an act of preservation, a collective promise to protect the wild beauty that remains.

On our final morning, I woke to a chorus of bird calls weaving through the mist that hugged the treetops. The air felt charged with anticipation, as if the land itself wanted to leave us with one last gift. We set off on a guided walk, our steps softened by the damp forest floor. I held my breath as we stumbled upon a family of western lowland gorillas, their dark eyes reflecting curiosity rather than fear. It was a fleeting connection, but it filled me with a sense of reverence I hadn't anticipated.

We spent our last afternoon on the beach, watching the ocean's waves lap at the footprints left by forest elephants. I marveled at the sight—elephants on a beach! It felt like a scene out of a dream, surreal and magical in its simplicity. The sun dipped lower, casting long shadows that stretched across the sand, and I realized how few places in the world allow such intimate encounters with nature, free from the crowds and the noise.

Gabon is not a place that serves itself up on a silver platter. It asks for patience, for curiosity, and for a willingness to embrace the unknown. But for those who do, it offers something far greater than photo opportunities or checklists.

It offers a chance to witness the world as it once was: wild, free, and teeming with life.

Imagine waking up to the soft hum of the jungle at dawn, sipping coffee as the mist rises off the lagoon, revealing the silhouettes of egrets gliding through the morning light. Picture yourself drifting through mangrove channels on a silent boat, where the splash of a breaching humpback whale could be your only company. Envision walking along a stretch of beach where your only footprints join those of the elusive sitatunga, sharing the shore with creatures who belong here far more than we ever will.

In Loango National Park, the boundaries between land and sea, between human and wild, blur into something indescribable. It's a place where you're reminded of your own smallness, yet feel deeply connected to something much bigger. Gabon doesn't just show you nature—it lets you feel it, in every breath of fresh air, every rustle in the undergrowth, and every heartbeat that echoes your own.

So, if you're looking for an adventure off the beaten path, where the wildlife outnumbers the people and every day is a lesson in humility, Gabon is waiting. It's a place for dreamers and doers, for those who crave something real and unfiltered. And if you let it, this wild, wonderful country will leave its mark on your soul—just as it has on mine.

Chapter IX

SOUTH SUDAN

November 2023

Life is either a daring adventure or nothing at all.

– Helen Keller

South Sudan doesn't just sit on the map; it perches in your mind, an idea of resilience wrapped in red dust, endless skies, and the hum of possibility. It's the world's youngest country, born in 2011 after a brutal 21-year war for independence, and yet, the spirit here feels older than time—raw, unbroken, and untamed.

Juba, the capital, greeted me with a sensory assault in the best way possible. Picture this: bustling streets filled with tuk-tuks dodging potholes as if it were a competitive sport, a marketplace so alive it almost seemed to breathe, and the unmistakable smell of roasting peanuts mixed with the sharp tang of freshly chopped wood. At every corner, there was movement—a woman balancing an impossible load of bananas on her head, a barefoot boy expertly kicking a punctured football, and the chatter that feels like a song you don't know the words to but hum along with it anyway.

The marketplace was chaos distilled into beauty. Stalls spilled over with kitenge fabrics in colors so bold they could make a rainbow blush. Mangoes stacked like small pyramids gleamed in the golden light, and wooden carvings of cattle—the symbol of wealth, pride, and life here—seemed to watch me from every angle. I moved slowly, taking it all in, knowing that in places like this, it's the small moments that hit the hardest: the shared laugh over my clumsy attempt at Dinka phrases, the toddler who tugged at my sleeve, curious about my camera, the vendor who waved me over just to share a slice of papaya. This wasn't the South Sudan I had read about in news stories. This was a place with grit, hustle, and so much life it was impossible to look away.

But Juba was just the prelude. Armed with a restless curiosity and a backpack full of hope, I was ready to venture solo into South Sudan's heartland to meet the Mundari tribe—a community whose way of life feels like something out of an ancient epic. Imagine a world where cattle are more than animals; they're currency, status, companions, and even mythology wrapped in flesh and horns. With nearly 750,000 members, the Mundari form one of South Sudan's largest ethnic groups, and their connection to their cattle isn't just practical—it's almost spiritual.

Here, under skies so wide they make you feel like you've stepped into infinity, the rhythm of life beats to the steady hum of grazing herds. Every action, every tradition, every whispered song seems to orbit around these majestic creatures, their curved horns slicing through the horizon like proud monuments to a way of life that refuses to fade. I wasn't just stepping into their land; I was stepping into their story—one that had endured centuries of upheaval and yet remained unshaken, vibrant, and deeply tied to the earth.

I had read about the Mundari for years, fascinated by their ancient customs, their starkly beautiful landscapes, and the surreal imagery of men standing guard over herds of long-horned cattle under smoke-filled skies. For them, cattle aren't just a livelihood; they're an identity, a way of life passed down through generations like a sacred thread.

Getting there wasn't easy—and that was part of the appeal. South Sudan doesn't roll out the red carpet for travelers. It challenges you. There are no cute boutique hotels or Instagram-ready cafes serving overpriced lattes. Here, every moment feels earned, and I was ready to dive in, dust-covered boots and all.

This trip was about connection—about standing on soil that had endured so much and still found a way to bloom. The Mundari were waiting, and I couldn't wait to see what stories they had to tell.

Mundari Tribe

A Symphony of Cattle and Culture

Long before the sun rose, I found myself on the bumpy road to one of the most isolated and fascinating corners of South Sudan. The Mundari, an ancient pastoralist tribe, had long captivated my imagination. Their entire world orbits their cattle—a sacred bond that blurs the line between survival and spirituality. Heading toward their remote village felt like chasing a secret, one whose essence could never fully be captured in photos or words but demanded to be felt firsthand.

The jeep jolted and swayed as we left Juba's relative bustle far behind. My guide—a stoic man with a wry smile—offered tidbits about the Mundari as we drove. "Their cows are like gods," he said, gesturing broadly at the vast, open land. "No cattle, no life."

By the time we arrived, the air had shifted. Smoke rose in delicate spirals from small fires scattered across the settlement, mingling with the musky, earthy scent of cattle. The village seemed to pulse with life, a rhythm dictated by the hum of cows, the laughter of children, and the quiet focus of daily chores.

The Mundari people emerged to greet us. Women, draped in vivid, sun-soaked fabrics, approached with shy curiosity. Their skin glistened in the sunlight, and their tattoos—geometric designs etched with precision—stood out as marks of beauty and identity. "This," one woman said, gesturing to the intricate lines across her arms, "is my story." Her pride was evident, her smile warm.

Children zipped past in a blur of energy, already at work despite their tender ages. Boys no older than five wielded herding sticks like seasoned cowboys, guiding massive Ankole cattle whose horns arched into the sky like works of art. Girls carried wooden buckets, ready to collect milk, their tiny frames belied by their obvious sense of purpose. For the Mundari, childhood is not an idle phase but a time to learn, to contribute, to live as an integral part of the community.

The village revolved around its herd. The cattle—each one named, known, and cherished—are everything to the Mundari. Their milk sustains, their hides protect, their dung fuels fires and builds shelters. Even their ash, gathered after burning dung, serves as mosquito repellent for both people and livestock. Watching the Mundari tend to their animals was like witnessing a sacred dance – their movements were careful, reverent, and deeply interconnected with the rhythm of life around them.

Mid-morning brought a break in the routine, and I found myself drawn into conversations with the men of the tribe. They proudly shared stories about their cattle, each animal's lineage recounted as though it were part of the family tree. "This one," a young man said, pointing to a particularly regal cow, "saved my brother's life when we had to cross a river." Another boasted about his herd's strength during a season of drought, his words tinged with both pride and gratitude.

As the sun climbed higher, a sudden downpour swept across the landscape, drenching the village in minutes. The cattle, undisturbed, gathered beneath the sprawling branches of acacia trees, their horns creating a surreal silhouette against the stormy sky. The Mundari took shelter in their huts, built from mud and thornbush, their thatched roofs weathering the rain with ease.

I was invited into one of these huts, where a woman handed me a gourd of fresh milk as a gesture of hospitality. Though I declined the offering out of caution, I was moved by the gesture's intimacy.

When the rain ceased, the village came alive again. The cattle were herded back into the open pastures, and preparations began for the evening rituals. I was ushered toward an open clearing where the men engaged in wrestling matches, a tradition as old as the tribe itself. They grappled with a mix of strength and playfulness, their laughter punctuating the air. Nearby, the women tended to small fires, their hair styled in intricate *duku* shapes, each one a masterpiece in its own right.

As the sun dipped low, casting a fiery glow over the savanna, I found myself seated around the communal fire. The day's work gave way to quiet conversations, laughter, and a shared sense of peace.

One elder leaned toward me, his voice soft but firm. "Our cattle are our life. If they thrive, so do we. When the gods give you something so precious, you care for it like your child."

The beauty of the Mundari's life lies in its unyielding simplicity and its unbreakable bonds. Every task, every ritual, every moment is woven with intention and respect. To an outsider, it may seem harsh—a life dictated by the needs of cattle and the unpredictability of nature. But for the Mundari, it is a life of purpose, of connection, of resilience.

As I lay under a blanket of stars that night, the lowing of cattle and the distant hum of voices lulling me to sleep, I realized I had witnessed something rare: a people living not in spite of nature but as part of it. The Mundari had shared their world with me, and in doing so, they had left an indelible mark on my own.

Final Reflections

South Sudan – A Land Misunderstood

South Sudan is not a postcard destination, nor does it try to be. It's raw, unpolished, and profoundly real—a place where life breathes in its most elemental form. Yet, as I prepared to leave, I felt as though I were parting from a long-lost friend. This land, so often reduced to headlines of conflict and chaos, had revealed to me a different truth: a story of resilience, grace, and quiet defiance.

Sitting by the campfire on my last night, surrounded by the Mundari's ash-dusted silhouettes, the world felt impossibly still. The sky stretched vast and infinite, the stars brighter than I'd ever seen, as if South Sudan had been holding its own constellation just for me. The rhythmic hum of the cattle blended with the soft murmur of voices—children giggling, elders sharing stories, warriors discussing tomorrow's tasks. It wasn't just peaceful; it was transcendent, a reminder of life stripped down to its most sacred connections.

The Mundari had taught me something profound, something I struggled to articulate even to myself: that strength is rooted in balance. The way they lived—harmoniously intertwined with their cattle and land—wasn't just survival; it was an act of quiet rebellion against a world that often values dominance over coexistence. Their reverence for the Ankole cattle wasn't quaint or naive; it was wisdom passed down through generations and a testament to the beauty of interdependence.

Watching the Mundari people tend to their cattle—a bond so sacred it feels like family—I was struck by how their rituals mirrored my own experiences growing up. And in those quiet, deliberate moments of care, I couldn't help but think of my family and the small, nurturing traditions we've held onto despite the distances and chaos of life.

For my family, it was always the simple things that kept us close. Growing up in a small, tight-knit household, it was just my mom, my brother, and me. Even now, after we've each built lives of our own, we make it a point to carve out time for one another—a trip together, a shared meal, or just the quiet joy of being in the same space. I've always cherished those moments, like watching my mom cook dishes that carry the taste of generations. Her sambar, rich and comforting, feels like a thread connecting me to my grandmother, to a long line of women who expressed love through the act of nurturing.

My grandparents, too, built connections through rituals. When I was an undergraduate in India, far from my parents who lived in Muscat, my weekends were spent with my grandparents. They would wait eagerly for me to visit, handpicking festive dresses for me to wear and preparing feasts that seemed to overflow with their love. I can still picture my grandmother's face lighting up as I took my first bite of the meal she'd carefully prepared. These weren't just acts of care—they were acts of identity, ways of reminding me who I was and where I came from, even in the midst of all the noise and change life brings.

Sitting with the Mundari by the campfire, I felt a deep sense of kinship, a recognition of the universality of nurturing traditions. Much like my family's rituals, the Mundari's care for their cattle wasn't just about survival—it was about connection. The way they spoke of their cattle, each one named and known, reminded me of the reverence with which my grandparents treated the rituals of our family. It's this reverence, I realized, that keeps us grounded and makes life feel sacred even in its most chaotic moments. There's a beauty in such rituals, in the way they anchor us to something larger than ourselves. For the Mundari, that anchor is their cattle. For me, it's the memory of my grandmother's hands deftly stirring spices into a pot, the sound of my grandfather's laughter as he teased me about how quickly I outgrew my dresses, and the sacred simplicity of those weekend visits. These moments remind us that nurturing is more than care—it's an act of identity, of ensuring that something of ourselves endures.

And just like the Mundari, who see their cattle through every stage of life until their death, I've learned to cherish the fleeting nature of time with those I love. As I've grown older and watched my parents age, I've come to understand the true value of these bonds. They're not grandiose or extravagant; they're the quiet, steady acts of love and care that make us human. The Mundari's connection to their cattle reminded me of my own family's ability to nurture one another, to find beauty in the mundane and the meaningful in the smallest of traditions.

Before I arrived, South Sudan loomed in my imagination as a place of danger. Stories of civil war, famine, and displacement had shaped my perception. But the people I met—the Mundari, the market vendors in Juba, the children racing across dirt roads with handmade toys—shattered those narratives. Their resilience wasn't something to pity; it was something to admire. They laughed freely, loved deeply, and lived with a fierce commitment to the community that I found humbling. Travelers often speak of countries as though they exist to meet our expectations. South Sudan doesn't care what you want it to be. It simply is. Its beauty is unapologetically wild—vast grasslands, thick swamps teeming with life, and skies that stretch endlessly. There's no curated experience, no safety net of tourism infrastructure. It's not a destination that will roll out the red carpet; instead, it holds out a hand and invites you to walk alongside it, to listen, to see.

Leaving South Sudan wasn't easy. As the plane took off, I pressed my face to the window, desperate to hold onto the sight of the landscape: the Nile cutting through emerald plains, the clusters of huts dotting the countryside, the faint traces of campfire smoke rising into the dawn. This wasn't a farewell; it was a promise to carry this place with me, to tell its story differently than it's been told before.

South Sudan is young, yes—but in its youth lies ancient wisdom. It is a country still finding its footing, yet its people have stood tall for generations. They have endured storms that would have shattered others, and still, they offer warmth, hospitality, and hope to strangers like me. So, to the skeptics, the cautious, and the curious: South Sudan isn't just safe—it's alive in ways that defy expectation. It won't hand you comfort on a platter, but it will feed your soul. It will challenge you to confront your assumptions, to sit with discomfort, and to see beauty in its most unvarnished form.

As I left, I couldn't help but reflect on the mantra that had brought me here in the first place: *Why not?* It's a question that had opened doors I didn't know existed, a compass that had guided me to one of the most transformative journeys of my life.

For the traveler seeking not just a destination but a revelation, South Sudan awaits. It will unsettle you, inspire you, and stay with you long after you've gone. And in that pursuit of "why not?" you may just find a version of yourself you didn't know was waiting to be discovered.

LEAST VISITED AND SOUL FILLED

Sudan | Turkmenistan | Sao Tome and Principe | Comoros

Chapter X

SUDAN

January 2023

> ***The question isn't who's going to let me; it's who's going to stop me.***
>
> ***– Ayn Rand***

Sudan—once Africa's largest country before its borders shifted in 2011. Today, it remains a place of deep complexity, a mosaic woven together by a tumultuous past and a vibrant cultural heritage that defies easy categorization. Mention Sudan, and the immediate response is often one of concern: "How did you even get in?" It's a fair question given the nation's media portrayal, dominated by conflict and war. But like many of the places I've ventured into, Sudan's true essence lies beyond the headlines, in stories etched into its land and whispered through its people.

Standing in the shadows of the Pyramids of Meroë, I could feel the ancient pulse of the Kingdom of Kush. These aren't the grand, polished pyramids of Egypt that fill our history books; they are smaller, steeper, but every bit as majestic. Over 200 pyramids scatter the Nubian Desert, some half-buried by golden sand, as if still guarding secrets from centuries ago. To touch the stone walls of these pyramids is to bridge a gap across time, to sense the same arid breeze that once carried the voices of pharaohs and traders who thrived here.

It's in moments like these that the narrative of Sudan transforms. It's not just a country marked by political strife—it's a land brimming with contrasts. On one side, the sprawling desert stretches out like a vast, sunlit canvas. On the other, the Nile River snakes through the landscape, a ribbon of life that nourishes the soil and the spirit. Along its banks, greenery bursts forth, giving rise to towns where life buzzes with a distinct rhythm. In Omdurman, the largest souq in the country, I wandered through a maze of stalls. The air was heavy with the scent of cinnamon, cloves, and dried hibiscus flowers. Vendors, with voices roughened by years of bargaining, called out their wares in a lively chorus, their enthusiasm as vibrant as the spices on display.

"Did you try the foul medames?" a beaming vendor asked, gesturing to a steaming pot of fava beans. I smiled, feeling a pang of nostalgia. Growing up in the Middle East, this humble dish had been a staple of my childhood. Still, I nodded eagerly. "It's our breakfast favorite," he insisted, ladling a generous serving onto a plate for me. It felt like an invitation, a small yet significant gesture of Sudanese hospitality that spoke volumes.

The deeper I traveled, the more I realized that Sudan's richness isn't confined to its ancient relics or bustling markets. It's in its people—a tapestry of over 500 ethnic groups, each thread adding a unique hue to the fabric of the nation. Here, Arabic mingles with the melodic tones of Nubian, Beja, and countless other indigenous languages. My guide, Khalid, was a walking encyclopedia of local knowledge. As we strolled through Khartoum's streets, he pointed out the cultural nuances that shape everyday life. "Sudan is a melting pot," he said with a smile. "It's not just one culture—there's the Nubian legacy in the north, the rich traditions of the Beja, and the diverse tapestry of Darfur."

He paused as we passed a local mosque, where a group of men were beginning their sufi dance, their bodies swaying in a trance-like rhythm. I watched, transfixed by the movement and the spiritual intensity that radiated from them. "Like what?" I asked, eager to understand more about the different cultural influences that Khalid spoke of.

"Well," he continued thoughtfully, "take Nubian music—it's distinct, filled with the sound of ancient drums and lyres. And in Darfur, art is more than just decoration; it's a form of storytelling, passed down through generations." His voice held a quiet pride.

Sudan is a land of staggering diversity—both in its people and its landscapes. The Red Sea coast glistens like a sapphire under the sun, its coral reefs alive with vibrant marine life, drawing divers from across the globe. But travel just a few hundred miles inland, and you'll find the endless dunes of the Sahara, where solitude reigns and the horizon stretches infinitely. It's this contrast that makes Sudan so compelling. One moment you're submerged in the underwater wonders of Port Sudan, and the next, you're gazing at the rolling dunes, feeling like you've stepped onto another planet.

Here, history isn't just something to be read about in books; it's alive, breathing through the streets, the landscapes, and the people who inhabit them. In Sudan, I didn't just find a misunderstood nation; I found a place that made me question my own assumptions, a land that challenged me to look beyond the surface and find the stories hidden beneath.

Khartoum

The very name conjures a blend of ancient echoes and modern energy, a city in flux yet grounded in the enduring strength of its people. The sun-drenched city pulsed with a warmth that reached beyond the heat—its essence seeped into every alley, every face, every breath. The chaos, the colors, the sounds—all coalesced into something beautiful and raw. It was a place that whispered, screamed and embraced all at once.

Children darted through the crowded markets like sparks from a fire, their laughter a melody I couldn't help but carry with me. It was the kind of joy that caught you off guard—the kind that told you that, despite everything, life here was lived fully, passionately, unabashedly. Vendors shouted their offerings above the hum of voices, their faces alive with the pride of their craft. "Look there," Khalid's voice broke through the sounds, his finger pointing toward a narrow alleyway.

The walls were alive with murals—bursting with color, with emotion, with the history of a people who had long been misunderstood. Each stroke, each symbol, each face on those walls spoke volumes. Some murals depicted figures from Sudan's ancient past, the iconic Nubian queens and mighty kings whose legacies still lingered in the sands of time. Others celebrated the quiet, often overlooked beauty of daily Sudanese life. The simple elegance of a woman's scarf fluttering in the breeze. A young man's face lit with the joy of dance. I stepped closer, running my fingers over the textured surfaces, feeling the stories as though the wall itself were breathing with the city. I could almost hear the pulse of life—the heartbeat of Khartoum—embedded in those murals. "This is where artists express themselves," Khalid said softly.

We wandered deeper into the market, a labyrinth of stalls spilling over with vibrantly fresh produce, spices so potent they could almost intoxicate you, and handcrafted goods that spoke of generations of skill passed down like secrets. The air was thick with the scent of grilled kebabs crackling over an open flame, and the sweet, intoxicating fragrance of pastries drenched in honey. I could taste the city in the air, and my heart fluttered in response.

Khalid nudged me toward a stall, his finger pointing at the golden, crispy sambusas being piled high. "Try that," he urged with a grin. The pastry cracked under my teeth as I bit into it, releasing the rich warmth of spiced potatoes and peas. The flavors were vibrant, alive, almost rebellious. I could feel it in every bite—the spirit of Sudan itself, daring to be tasted, to be savored. "You haven't tasted Sudan until you've had street food," Khalid chuckled, his eyes twinkling with the knowledge that comes from a lifetime of calling this place home.

Moving through the streets, I found myself captivated by the contrasting pulse of Khartoum. The modern skyscrapers rose with defiance against the skyline, their glass and steel exteriors reflecting the fierce sun. Yet they stood in harmony with the old, the sacred. The towering minarets of mosques seemed to reach toward the heavens, their call to prayer a sacred melody that filled the air with both reverence and defiance. The city, in its beautiful dissonance, was a symphony of tradition and modernity.

"Over there is the National Museum," Khalid gestured toward a grand building that stood as a silent sentinel of history. I could feel my pulse quicken at the sight of it. Ancient treasures, relics of an empire that spanned centuries, sat within those walls—Pharaonic tombs, Nubian statues, all carefully preserved for a world that often overlooked their significance. In that moment, I felt the weight of the past pushing through the present. The thought of stepping inside, to lose myself among the relics of those who once ruled and dreamed in this land, was intoxicating.

But there was more to Khartoum than just its history. It was the heart of Sudan, beating with a resilience born of survival, of hope, of an unshakable belief that tomorrow would always come.

"We must visit Omdurman next," Khalid said as we navigated through a sea of people crossing the street in a dance of their own.

"Omdurman?" I asked, intrigued.

"The largest market in Sudan," Khalid replied, a grin spreading across his face. "You can find everything here—from traditional garments to intricate jewelry. And the stories, well, they are endless."

Journey to Meroë

The ride from Khartoum to Meroë felt like stepping back in time. As Khalid expertly navigated the winding, dusty roads, I pressed my forehead against the cool glass window, absorbing the shifting landscapes outside. The urban hum of Khartoum slowly gave way to vast, arid plains, where acacia trees and resilient shrubs clung stubbornly to the earth, each one a testament to the harsh beauty of this land. Goats and camels grazed lazily by the roadside, reminders of a pastoral life that seemed almost untouched by the chaos of the city.

"Look," Khalid said, pointing ahead. "Those are Nubian villages." I followed his gesture, spotting clusters of mud-brick houses nestled under the sparse shade of palm trees. Children played with their toys, their laughter mingling with the wind, while women balanced water jugs on their heads with an effortless grace, their movements so fluid, so dignified, that even a yoga enthusiast would be envious.

Every so often, Khalid would share snippets of history, like breadcrumbs leading me closer to the treasure that was Meroë. "Did you know," he mused, "that these pyramids were part of the Kingdom of Kush, a rival to ancient Egypt? They were warriors, traders, and kings. They left their mark on the world."

Anticipation bubbled inside me with every mile we drove. I had seen pictures, read stories, but nothing could prepare me for that first, breathtaking view of the pyramids rising from the desert sands, their silhouettes cutting against the vast blue sky. It was as if time itself had stopped, holding its breath.

When we finally arrived, the pyramids stood majestic and stoic, as if guarding centuries of secrets. Unlike the famous pyramids of Giza, these were smaller, steeper, fewer in number—but their elegance and mystery were undeniable. They felt surreal, otherworldly, and they commanded respect with a quiet power. I pitched my tent right in front of them—a small, modern shelter juxtaposed against these grand relics of the past. As I hammered in the last peg, I caught Khalid watching me, a knowing smile playing at the corners of his lips.

"Excited?" he asked.

"More than I can put into words," I replied. There's a particular thrill that comes from standing so close to something ancient, something that has endured the test of time and yet still quietly stands, unmoved.

As dusk fell, the sky bloomed into hues of orange and purple, painting the landscape with colors so vivid they almost seemed unreal. The world around me quieted as the pyramids stood, unmoving. I zipped up my tent, leaving a small opening to peek out at the breathtaking view, my heart swelling with gratitude.

The stars began to twinkle one by one, small pinpricks of light scattered across a velvet canvas, beckoning me into the vastness of the universe. I lay on my back, my heart racing with the rare opportunity to be alone with history, enveloped in a serenity that felt almost otherworldly. This vastness, this magical space packed with history and wonder, felt like it was just for me.

Morning arrived slowly, soft light filtering through the fabric of my tent as dawn broke, casting a warm glow over the world. I emerged into a landscape bathed in gold, the sunbeams illuminating the pyramids in a way that made them shimmer with life, each ray revealing a new dimension of their grandeur. I stood in awe, captivated as daylight unveiled every crevice and shadow, breathing in the significance of the moment.

Khalid stood nearby, watching the scene with quiet reverence. “Incredible, isn’t it?” he whispered, almost afraid that speaking too loudly might shatter the fragile silence.

I nodded, too overwhelmed to speak. I had read about the pyramids, seen pictures, but standing here—seeing them in person, so peaceful, so untouched—it was a different experience altogether. It felt like standing in a sacred space, where time had paused to let me take it all in.

Meroë's Hidden Legacy

These pyramids were built between 300 BC and 350 AD as tombs for the Kushite kings and queens. Unlike their Egyptian counterparts, they possessed steeper angles and were smaller in size, yet still radiated an air of majesty that left me utterly speechless. They were a juxtaposition of strength and elegance that transcended time. Arriving in Sudan, I was struck by its quiet grandeur. These weren't just monuments—they were storytellers, keepers of an ancient civilization that thrived here long before the modern borders of Sudan were drawn.

I couldn't help but marvel at the ingenuity of the Kushite civilization. These pyramids weren't built to impress or outdo others but to honor their people and the land they belonged to. Their steep, elegant angles mirrored the dignity of a culture that valued permanence and purpose. It made me think about the impermanence of much of what we create today. What would endure of our time? What legacies would we leave behind?

The pyramids reminded me that even in a world consumed by conflict and change, some things can stand firm, provided they are built with intention and respect for the environment around them.

Meroë is home to more than forty pyramids, the remnants of royal lineage buried beneath their stones, their stories waiting to be rediscovered. The air seemed to hum with their ancient voices, whispering tales of glory, ambition, and a people whose legacy was too often forgotten.

"They say each pyramid is a story," Khalid said, his eyes sparkling with enthusiasm, "waiting for someone curious enough to listen." And there I stood, an Indian woman in the middle of a land that wasn't mine, amidst centuries-old structures, believing that curiosity triumphs over everything else. I was a bridge between my world and the ancient echoes that still resonated here. As we prepared to leave Meroë behind, I glanced back one last time at the mighty pyramids, my heart filled with a sense of reverence and awe that would stay with me forever.

A Journey Beyond Fear

When I first decided to travel to Sudan, I was driven by an irresistible pull of curiosity—an unshakable need to see the untold stories hidden beneath its desert sands. Unlike the Egyptian pyramids that dominate history books and Instagram feeds, the pyramids of Meroë remained almost unheard of, even among my most seasoned travel companions. I was astonished by how little people knew about these stunning structures—over 200 of them scattered across the Nubian Desert, steeper and more intimate than their Egyptian counterparts, yet just as majestic.

But I'd be lying if I said curiosity alone brought me to Sudan. There was hesitation, too—a gnawing fear rooted in the stories we've all been told. Sudan is often reduced to a single narrative of conflict and instability, its people overshadowed by stark headlines and devastating imagery. For years, even I had unconsciously accepted these portrayals. But the more I learned about the country, the more I realized how much of its richness, its resilience, and its humanity was being left out.

The challenge, I knew, wasn't just logistical—it was personal. I had to confront my own preconceptions and fears. Traveling to Sudan wasn't going to be about checking off another destination; it was about looking beyond the surface, pushing through the noise of stereotypes, and letting the country tell its own story.

But it wasn't just the ancient monuments that left an indelible mark on me. It was the people. Every interaction, every smile, every shared story brought Sudan to life in a way no photograph ever could.

The Sudanese people are deeply proud of their history and culture, and they carry that pride with quiet strength. Despite hardships most of us can't imagine, they radiate warmth, generosity, and a deep sense of community. I remember a vendor at a market offering me a taste of tamarind juice with a smile so genuine it felt like a gift. I remember the children laughing and playing in alleyways painted with murals of hope and resilience. And I remember the hauntingly beautiful rhythms of the Sufi dancers, their movements pulling fragments of the past into the present.

Final Thoughts

As I write this, the whispers of Meroë linger in my memory, and I am filled with a bittersweet ache recalling my trip to Sudan, just before the conflict erupted.

I was initially drawn to Sudan because of something few in my travel circle knew: the existence of the mirror pyramids of Meroë. While the Egyptian pyramids capture global fascination, I found myself captivated by the hundreds more that quietly stand in Sudan, bearing witness to an ancient civilization that predates turmoil. It surprised me that a country so often reduced to images of conflict held such profound historical treasures. In my own mind, I realized I had unconsciously allowed these narratives of instability to obscure the deeper truth of Sudan's culture and heritage. I knew I had to see it for myself, to confront these assumptions head-on and uncover the reality of a place that deserves so much more than the world's indifference.

"People need to see this," I murmured to Khalid, as we walked through Khartoum's vibrant markets, pausing to admire murals splashed with hopeful colors against the city's worn walls. He nodded, his expression a mix of pride and sorrow.

"They need to understand what this country really offers," he said, gazing toward the horizon where the sun's golden light kissed the ancient pyramids, casting long shadows over the desert sands. "It's easy for them to judge without knowing. They hear about conflict and shut their minds."

Sudanese history is incredible, yet often overlooked. The people I met carried an immense pride in their heritage, one that transcends the challenges they've faced. Despite their struggles, they radiate a warmth and generosity that left an indelible mark on me. I stood in awe before the pyramids of Meroë at sunrise, surrounded by hundreds of these ancient structures, utterly alone in a landscape that felt otherworldly. Unlike the throngs of tourists crowding the sites of Egypt, here I found a sacred stillness—a rare moment where I could truly feel the weight of history and the timeless endurance of this land. It was surreal, a memory that I will carry with me forever.

In that silence, I understood what Sudanese resilience truly means. It's the shopkeeper offering a taste of tamarind juice with a smile, the children laughing in alleyways painted with murals of freedom, the hauntingly beautiful rhythms of the Sufi dancers pulling fragments of the past into the present. It's the strength of a people who have weathered unimaginable hardships yet choose to celebrate life in small but significant ways. Their smiles aren't born of naivety—they are acts of defiance, tiny flames of hope that refuse to be extinguished.

This journey became a powerful reminder of the transformative power of travel, especially to places that are misunderstood or rarely visited. It changes you, not just because of the sights, but because of the deeper connection you form when you look beyond the surface. These century-old structures have stood the test of time, and so have the people who keep their stories alive, even as their land is torn apart by conflict.

The reality of Sudan hit me hardest after I left, when I learned of the war that broke out just three months after my visit. I think back to the moments I shared with Khalid, to our quiet conversations filled with dreams of a peaceful Sudan. It feels surreal, almost cruel, to have experienced this place at a time of relative calm, unaware of the storm brewing on the horizon. It's a stark reminder of the fragility of peace and the urgency of sharing these stories now, before they're lost in the chaos of war.

"Sudan is alive with history," I had said, feeling the weight of those words. I felt an overwhelming sense of responsibility, a pull to share these experiences—the laughter of children in bustling streets, the fragrant spices filling my senses at market stalls, the awe-inspiring grandeur of pyramids standing resilient against time's passage. "This land deserves another chance," I affirmed to Khalid and to myself. "And so do its people."

Khalid's words lingered with me: "Once peace returns, travelers will discover a land filled with warmth and hospitality." It's a sentiment that ignites something within me, a determination to advocate for Sudan, to inspire others to see the beauty that lies beneath. I want people to arrive not just as tourists but as friends, ready to embrace new experiences, open to the unexpected, and willing to witness a Sudan that is so much more than its conflicts.

As I ready my pen to continue telling these stories, I whisper a quiet promise to Sudan and to all the misunderstood places of the world: "Let's tell their story."

Travel Note: How to Reach Meroë

If my words have sparked even a flicker of curiosity in you, here's how you can plan your own journey to Meroë.

1. **Getting There**
   Most travelers fly into Khartoum. While there are no direct international flights from most major cities, Khartoum is accessible via connecting flights through cities like Cairo, Addis Ababa, and Istanbul. Once you arrive, the best way to reach Meroë is by car. The journey takes about 5-6 hours, and while there are buses, it's highly recommended to hire a guide who can navigate the rural roads and offer invaluable insights into the local culture. Sudan's tourism infrastructure is still developing, so a local guide enhances the experience significantly, making it smoother and richer.

2. **Visa and Permits**
   Most nationalities will require a visa to enter Sudan. The process isn't complicated, but you'll need to apply for your visa in advance. You can either apply through the Sudanese embassy or consulate in your country or use an online visa service. Make sure to check the latest entry requirements, as they can change. Additionally, certain areas around Meroë may require special permits to visit, which your guide can help secure in advance.

3. Local Etiquette

Sudan is a conservative country, and it's important to respect local customs and dress modestly. This is especially true in rural areas where traditional values are more pronounced. Women should cover their shoulders and knees, and men should avoid wearing shorts in more conservative regions. Understanding and respecting these cultural norms will not only enrich your experience but will also help you connect with the locals in a deeper way.

4. Safety

While Sudan has experienced significant political and social unrest in recent years, many parts of the country, including Khartoum and Meroë, are relatively safe to visit with proper precautions. That said, it's crucial to stay informed about the local situation before traveling. Register with your embassy, keep an eye on travel advisories, and always listen to the advice of your guide. Trust your instincts and always err on the side of caution. Travel in groups if possible, and never venture into unfamiliar areas without guidance.

Chapter XI

TURKMENISTAN

April 2023

> ***I see my path, but I don't know where it leads. Not knowing where I'm going is what inspires me to travel it.***
>
> **– *Rosalia de Castro***

Turkmenistan—a country so veiled in mystery it feels almost mythical. Tucked away in Central Asia, this landlocked nation shares borders with Iran, Afghanistan, Uzbekistan, and Kazakhstan. It stretches into the vastness of the Karakum Desert, an endless sea of golden sand, where ancient trade routes once buzzed with life. To the west, it kisses the Caspian Sea, its coastline a serene counterpoint to the arid expanse inland.

This is a place often left out of glossy travel guides and bucket lists, a country so sparsely visited that even seasoned explorers raise their eyebrows at its mention. Turkmenistan welcomes fewer tourists annually than the Louvre does in a day, making it one of the least explored countries on earth. But for those willing to peer beyond its enigmatic reputation, Turkmenistan offers an experience like no other—a story written in marble, sand, and fire.

My journey to Turkmenistan began, fittingly, with a challenge—the visa. Imagine the bureaucratic equivalent of scaling Mount Everest. Endless forms, a required invitation from a local agency, and an opaque approval process that seemed more about patience than practicality. It felt less like obtaining permission to visit a country and more like being initiated into a secret society. Each form signed, each document submitted was a step closer to unlocking the mysteries of a land few have walked.

When I finally stepped off the plane in Ashgabat, the capital city, I was greeted by a surreal landscape that looked like it belonged more in a sci-fi movie than reality. Nicknamed the "City of White Marble," Ashgabat holds a Guinness World Record for having the most marble-clad buildings in the world. Everything gleamed under the sun—government buildings, hotels, even lampposts. It was a city where extravagance and eccentricity collided, creating a skyline that felt both futuristic and oddly nostalgic. But beneath the glimmering surface lay a reality that was harder to grasp. Internet access was almost nonexistent, with social media platforms blocked and the web monitored like a hawk guarding its nest. Conversations felt stripped down to essentials, communication distilled into its purest form. In many ways, it reminded me of the stories I'd heard about North Korea.

Yet, as I sipped tea with an elderly man at a modest café that first evening, I discovered a truth that no firewall could hide. "You are brave," he told me, his voice tinged with humor as he nodded toward my camera. "Or foolish," I quipped, earning a laugh that seemed to bridge the chasm between our worlds.

Turkmenistan, I quickly realized, is a land of contrasts. It is a place where the starkness of government control exists alongside the warmth of its people. Where the flame-filled Darvaza Gas Crater—aptly nicknamed the "Gates of Hell"—burns day and night, a testament to nature's untamed power. Where ancient ruins like Merv, once one of the great cities of the Silk Road, whisper tales of empires long gone. It is also a country where traditions run deep. Turkmen carpets, woven with intricate patterns and vibrant colors, are more than just floor coverings—they are cultural heirlooms. Horse racing, an age-old sport, draws crowds under a blistering sun, their cheers echoing across the desert.

Each interaction here felt like a small rebellion against the narrative of oppression. A smile, a shared meal, a story told in hushed tones—these were acts of quiet defiance that revealed the soul of Turkmenistan. Traveling here is like peeling back the layers of an intricate tapestry. On the surface, you see control, extravagance, and isolation. But look deeper, and you find resilience, creativity, and a culture that refuses to be extinguished.

As I wandered through Ashgabat's marble streets, explored the ruins of Merv, and stood before the fiery gates of Darvaza,

I felt the weight of this country's history and the lightness of its spirit. Turkmenistan doesn't offer itself up easily. But for those who persist, it reveals something rare and unforgettable: a glimpse into the beauty of the hidden and the resilience of the human spirit.

Weaving Identity

From the moment I arrived in Turkmenistan, I felt enveloped in a world stitched together by tradition. The women wove with a precision that felt almost sacred, their actions deliberate and measured, as if each knot tied them closer to their ancestors.

It was impossible not to wonder what these rituals meant to them. As a self-proclaimed feminist, I felt an initial dissonance. Were these acts of cultural reverence or quiet submission? My thoughts drifted back to my time in Afghanistan, where the weight of societal expectations on women was suffocating, the oppression unmistakable. But Turkmenistan wasn't Afghanistan. Here, the customs, while deeply patriarchal, carried an elegance and grace that felt less like chains and more like roots. I couldn't help but think of India, of the rituals and roles that have shaped my own heritage. The parallels were unmistakable. Just as Indian traditions often delineate the roles of men and women, so too did Turkmen society. Yet, watching these women, I sensed pride rather than restraint, autonomy instead of confinement. They served tea with an artistry that elevated the ordinary, their movements imbued with a quiet power. Their carpets, masterpieces of color and design, weren't just objects—they were expressions of identity, shields of tradition in a world that seemed determined to unravel it all.

After I spent more time observing and listening, I realized that strength doesn't always look the way we expect. It doesn't always rebel or roar; sometimes, it is silent and steadfast. These women weren't questioning their traditions, nor did they seem concerned with the world beyond their borders—a world they largely couldn't access. With no internet, no intrusion of global modernity, their universe was self-contained, defined by customs and history. And perhaps, in that self-containment, there was freedom.

The carpets they wove told me as much about their world as their words did. They weren't trapped; they were preserving. And as I watched them work, I realized that my role as a traveler wasn't to impose my lens on their lives but to honor their choices, to carry their stories forward without judgment. In Turkmenistan, I learned that strength takes on forms as intricate and unexpected as a Turkmen carpet. It doesn't have to fit into the molds we recognize. It can be quiet, rooted, and deeply tied to a sense of identity that we, as outsiders, can only begin to understand. My task wasn't to find answers or redefine their choices but to leave with their stories woven into the fabric of my own journey.

Ashgabat... *A Marble Dream in the Desert*

"Welcome to the whitest city in the world," I muttered under my breath as we stepped into Ashgabat. It wasn't hyperbole. The city shimmered under the relentless desert sun, its skyline dominated by buildings draped in white marble, as if someone had handed an artist a blank canvas and said, *Go wild*.

Here, nothing is done halfway. Ashgabat doesn't flirt with grandeur—it marries it, puts it on a pedestal, and then sets the pedestal on fire for dramatic effect. Everywhere I looked, there were marble towers gleaming against the sapphire sky, their surfaces so polished they might as well have been mirrors reflecting dreams of ambition. It's a city that holds a Guinness World Record for the most marble buildings per square meter—a testament to human ingenuity and, let's be honest, an insatiable love for the dramatic.

But Ashgabat isn't just a city of shiny facades; it's a city of paradoxes. Beneath the marble gleam lies a layer of mystery and control. There's a strict rule that only white or light-colored cars are allowed on its streets. Imagine buying your dream red convertible, only to be told you'd need a fresh coat of white paint before you could drive it here. It's the kind of quirk that feels almost whimsical until you remember it's the law. But in that quirk lies the charm of Ashgabat—it unapologetically is what it is, and that makes it fascinating.

We began our exploration at the Independence Monument, a towering symbol of Turkmen pride. Golden gargoyles stood guard around its base, while the statue of Saparmurat Niyazov—the first president of independent Turkmenistan—reigned above. The sheer scale of it was overwhelming, its presence unmistakable as it cast long shadows across the plaza. Beside me, a local man caught my awestruck gaze and smiled. His posture straightened slightly, pride radiating from him as if the monument were a personal achievement.

Nearby, the 10 Horse Monument demanded attention. These golden sculptures of Akhal-Teke horses—a breed so prized they are called "the heavenly horses"—seemed to gallop against the blue expanse of the sky. Their intricate detailing captured every muscle and sinew, each figure poised mid-leap, defying time and gravity. While I was admiring them, I thought about how these horses embodied the spirit of Turkmenistan: enduring, graceful, and fiercely independent.

Our wanderings took us next to the Ministry of Knowledge, a building designed to resemble an open book. It felt both literal and poetic, a monument to learning that stood proudly in a city so rooted in its past yet eager to shape its future. "How do you think they teach here?" I asked my husband "With lots of whiteboards," he quipped, and we dissolved into laughter that echoed through the grand boulevards.

For lunch, we ventured into Sha Cafe, a cozy spot tucked away in Ashgabat's grandiose streets. The simplicity of the food was its magic—lentil soups rich with warmth, salads bursting with tangy flavors, and breads so fresh they practically melted in our mouths. Each bite felt like an introduction to the heart of Turkmen culture, where hospitality is served as generously as the portions.

Rejuvenated, we strolled through Inspiration Park, a green oasis amidst the city's marble. Fountains leapt and splashed in synchronized dances. Statues of ancient poets and philosophers stood sentinel, their faces carved with wisdom and wonder.

"Feeling inspired yet?" my friend asked, watching me take it all in.

"I feel like I've walked into a storybook," I said, and it wasn't an exaggeration.

As the sun dipped lower in the sky, we made our way to the Ertugrul Gazi Mosque, its domes glinting softly in the golden hour light. Its resemblance to Istanbul's Blue Mosque was undeniable, but what struck me most was the serenity. There were no throngs of tourists, no chatter or camera flashes. Just the sound of footsteps on stone, the soft murmur of prayers, and the gentle play of light filtering through intricate windows. It was a space that invited reflection—a reminder of the beauty that can be found in stillness.

And then there was the night. When the sun finally set, Ashgabat transformed. Its marble buildings, which had gleamed during the day, now glowed under vibrant neon lights. The streets seemed quieter, the air cooler, and the city felt almost dreamlike. We wandered without a plan, letting the gentle hum of the city guide us.

Ashgabat is not a city that reveals itself easily. It's layered, complex, and unapologetically unique. It challenges your assumptions and rewards your curiosity. Here, amidst the marble and the mystery, I found a place that wasn't just a stop on my journey—it was a chapter all its own.

In Ashgabat, I discovered that beauty doesn't always need explanation, and quirks can be the soul of a city. For all its grandeur, the heart of Turkmenistan's capital lies in its contrasts—where tradition meets modernity, and opulence dances with simplicity. It's a place that lingers in your mind long after you've left, urging you to peel back its layers again and again.

Here, under the vast Central Asian sky, I realized that travel isn't just about destinations—it's about the stories they tell and the questions they leave behind.

Erbent Village and the Saparmurat Hajji Mosque... *A Tapestry of Stories and Sand*

The morning greeted us with soft sunlight spilling over the endless desert, painting the Karakum's golden dunes in hues of warmth. Our destination was Darvaza, the infamous "Gateway to Hell," but first, a detour beckoned. Erbent Village—its name carried a promise of immersion into Turkmenistan's soul, a place where time seemed to slow and tradition thrived amidst the vast emptiness.

"Are you ready for some authentic Turkmen hospitality?" our guide asked.

The drive itself was a prelude to discovery. The road wove like a ribbon through the dunes, teasing us with glimpses of semi-nomadic life as it unfolded against the horizon. As we approached Erbent, I felt the rhythm of the place seep into my senses. This was no tourist attraction, but a living, breathing community where the past and present coexisted in harmony. The village unfurled before us like a canvas painted with vivid strokes: colorful yurts stood resolute against the sprawling plains, their fabric rippling gently in the breeze. Women adorned in flowing dresses of crimson and gold worked deftly on intricate carpets, their fingers moving in practiced patterns passed down through generations. Nearby, men tended to their flocks, the soft bleating of sheep mingling with the hum of the wind.

I was struck by the serenity of it all. Here, amidst the simplicity of life, was resilience—a community thriving in the face of nature's challenges. It felt as though we had stepped into a pocket of timelessness, where stories lived not in books but in the hands of artisans and the whispers of the land.

As we wandered deeper into the village, a small burial ground caught my eye. Its humble markers stood in stark contrast to the vastness around them, an unspoken reminder of history's weight. At its center, a lone nun stood, her figure framed by the blazing sun. She was a striking presence, cloaked in black and wrapped in quiet reverence. The graves she watched over belonged to soldiers who had perished during the Soviet-Afghan War—young men whose lives had been consumed by the tides of history.

Her presence was profound, almost sacred. She wasn't just standing over graves; she was standing over stories—of sacrifice, of conflict, of a time that had shaped Turkmenistan's identity in ways both visible and unseen.

"Do you think she knows their stories?" I whispered to my husband, struck by the quiet weight of her vigil.

"Maybe she's keeping their memories alive," he replied, his voice low and reflective.

It was a moment that lingered long after we left Erbent—a reminder that even in the remotest corners of the world, history breathes through the land and its people. Our journey continued toward the Saparmurat Hajji Mosque, a stark contrast to the village's humble charm. Rising from the desert with an air of grandeur, the mosque was a masterpiece of cross-cultural artistry. Its tiles, imported from Germany, shimmered like jewels under the midday sun. The ornate doors, brought from Morocco, stood as a testament to intricate craftsmanship. Built by a French company, the structure felt like a dialogue among nations, each element contributing to a unified vision.

"This feels like a mosaic of the world," I murmured, stepping inside and letting the cool air embrace me. The interior was just as breathtaking. Light poured through stained glass windows, casting vibrant patterns onto the polished floors. The air carried the faint scent of incense, mingling with the silence of the space. It wasn't just a mosque; it was a sanctuary of stories—of faith, of art, and of the interconnectedness that binds humanity.

From there, our guide took us to the Ruhy Mosque, a place that defied expectations. Built by Turkmenistan's former president, Saparmurat Niyazov, its scale was epic, its architecture grand, but its spirit felt curiously absent. Instead of Quranic verses adorning the columns, inscriptions from the president's book dominated the space—a shrine less to faith and more to the man himself. "This is definitely not your typical mosque," our guide quipped, a wry smile playing on his lips. It was, indeed, a peculiar place. Yet, even in its oddity, there was something to admire—a boldness, perhaps, in creating a structure that celebrated legacy over divinity. It was a stark reminder of the complexities of power and identity in Turkmenistan's modern history.

With the day drawing to a close, we resumed our journey toward Darvaza. The landscape began to shift around us, the soft undulations of desert giving way to an expanse that felt almost infinite. The sun, now lower in the sky, cast long shadows across the sand, its golden rays embracing the earth in a warm glow.

Excitement crackled in the air as we neared the infamous gas crater. It promised a spectacle like no other—flames that danced defiantly against the night, illuminating the desert with a fiery brilliance that felt both otherworldly and deeply primal. Each stop in Turkmenistan added a new color, a new texture to our journey—vibrant villages, breathtaking mosques, and landscapes that seemed to stretch beyond comprehension. And as we approached Darvaza, I couldn't help but feel that the best stories were the ones waiting to be uncovered, their truths hidden in the firelight of the unknown.

Darvaza... ***Standing at the Edge of Fire***

Darvaza, ominously nicknamed the "Gates of Hell," is neither a natural marvel nor a deliberate creation. It is, in fact, the result of a misstep—an ill-fated Soviet drilling experiment in 1971 that literally spiraled out of control. What was intended to be a quick fix for a collapsed natural gas field instead unleashed an eternal inferno. When the ground gave way, forming a massive crater, geologists decided to ignite the escaping gas, expecting it to burn out within a few days. Over fifty years later, the flames still rage, defying every effort to extinguish them.

Approaching Darvaza felt like stepping toward the end of the world. The barren desert stretched endlessly around us, its stillness interrupted only by the low, thunderous roar of the crater's fire. Even from a hundred meters away, you could feel its heat. Our home for the night was a yurt, a traditional circular dwelling that has stood the test of time across Central Asia. It was spacious yet intimate, its design both practical and inviting, with felt-lined walls that promised warmth as the desert's daytime heat gave way to its nighttime chill. I've always found something magical about yurts—they feel like a bridge between the ancient and the modern, a reminder of simpler times.

As night began to fall, the air around us shifted. The stars, one by one, emerged from the darkening sky, casting a celestial canopy over the desert. From the edge of the camp, the fiery glow of Darvaza lit the horizon, its light flickering across the sand like a beacon from another realm. The sight of the crater was breathtaking, almost surreal. Flames leapt and swirled from the depths, their movements hypnotic as they licked the walls of the crater in an unending dance.

"It's like the earth itself is alive," I whispered to my husband.

"Or fighting back," he replied, his voice tinged with awe.

Standing there, I felt both insignificant and invincible—a tiny figure on the edge of something vast and primal. The fire seemed to pulse with its own rhythm, a reminder of the earth's raw power and humanity's fleeting grasp over it.

Back at the camp, we settled around a small fire of our own, its modest crackling almost absurdly quaint compared to the roaring inferno nearby. Yet, in its simplicity, it brought a sense of connection. We shared stories, our laughter carried by the gentle desert breeze. The stars above seemed impossibly close, their light untouched by pollution or city glow, twinkling like they were in on our conversations.

Darvaza's full effect came alive at night. The crater glowed brighter, its flames casting an eerie yet mesmerizing light that transformed the desert into a realm out of legend. Shadows stretched and danced across the sand, painting the landscape with an otherworldly beauty. Camping here was not just a choice; it was essential to understanding the essence of this place. To feel the earth's heat beneath your feet, to hear the restless roar of the flames in the quiet of the desert night, to see the interplay of light and darkness—it was an experience that transcended mere sightseeing.

The next morning, the crater seemed calmer, its flames quieter under the sun's harsh glare. But the memory of that night lingered—a fiery spectacle and the vastness of the Karakum Desert etched into my mind.

Here, in this remote corner of Turkmenistan, where the ancient sands meet a modern marvel of miscalculation, I realized something: some places don't just leave you in awe—they demand you leave a part of yourself behind, as if the fire consumes not just gas, but a sliver of your soul.

Nokhur Valley... *A Portal to Timelessness*

The dusty, winding road felt like a thread unraveling as we journeyed into the heart of the Kopet Dag mountains. Rising defiantly between Turkmenistan and Iran, these rugged peaks seemed to beckon us into their embrace, their jagged edges etched against a cerulean sky. As our vehicle climbed higher, the arid plains gave way to verdant pockets of life—lush greenery clinging stubbornly to the mountainsides, as if defying the harshness of the land itself.

"Are you ready for this?" our guide asked.

"Absolutely," I replied, transfixed by the unfolding scenery. Each bend in the road revealed a new masterpiece of nature—deep shadows carving drama into the peaks, and splashes of earthy browns and vibrant greens painting the valleys below.

By the time we arrived in Nokhur Valley, it felt as though we had crossed an invisible threshold into another world. The air here carried a distinct energy, ancient and alive.

Everything about this place whispered of stories long told but not forgotten. Time seemed to stretch and twist, blending centuries of tradition into the present moment.

The village itself was a cluster of stone houses tucked against the mountains, their weathered walls standing like quiet sentinels guarding secrets passed through generations. As we parked near one of the oldest families in the village, the landscape seemed to sigh in welcome, its serenity wrapping around us. The family welcomed us with warmth so genuine it felt like being reunited with long-lost friends. Their home was a blend of simplicity and charm: long carpets spread across the floor, piled high with cushions that beckoned us to sit. Soon, plates of food began to appear—freshly baked bread, aromatic stews that filled the air with spices, and endless cups of steaming chai.

"This is how hospitality looks here," our host said with a smile, tearing into a piece of bread and gesturing for us to do the same.

As I watched the scene unfold, something curious caught my eye: the women covered their mouths with their headscarves whenever they spoke.

"Why do they do that?" I asked softly, not wanting to offend.

"It is a sign of reverence to the men," our guide explained, his tone neutral, as though presenting a fact rather than passing judgment.

I couldn't help but feel a twinge of discomfort, but it was tempered by the grace of these women. Later that afternoon, we wandered through Nokhur's cemetery—a place unlike any I'd seen before. Goat horns adorned the graves, each one a symbol of protection against evil spirits. Stones carved with steps seemed to promise a journey upward, guiding souls toward heaven. The air was thick with reverence, the stillness broken only by the soft rustle of the wind.

"This is incredible," I murmured, tracing my fingers over the weathered surface of a grave marker. "It feels... sacred."

"It is," our guide replied. "These traditions go back centuries, maybe even millennia."

The day wasn't done with surprises. A steep hike up to one of the valley's highest peaks awaited us. The climb tested every ounce of strength in my legs, the uneven trail winding ever upward. But each step brought new rewards: the crisp mountain air, the rustle of leaves whispering secrets, and the breathtaking panorama that unfolded when we finally reached the summit.

Standing there, the world below us seemed infinite. Valleys stretched like painted canvases, their colors shifting with the play of sunlight and shadow. It was a view that demanded silence, a moment too profound for words.

Final Thoughts... ***A Land of Contrasts and Quirks***

As we made our way back to Ashgabat, the journey still held one final gift: an underground cave with a lake said to possess healing properties. Descending hundreds of steps into the cool, dimly lit depths felt like entering another realm. The air grew cooler, the sound of our footsteps echoing faintly.

"Just wait until you see this," our guide said, his voice tinged with excitement.

When we reached the lake, it took my breath away. The water was impossibly clear, shimmering like liquid crystal under the faint light. It felt as though the earth itself had carved out this secret sanctuary, a place of quiet renewal hidden from the harshness above.

After the strenuous hike earlier in the day, stepping into the lake felt like a balm. Its cool embrace washed away fatigue, leaving me both energized and at peace. Driving back through the rugged landscapes of Turkmenistan, I reflected on the journey that had taken us from the gleaming marble of Ashgabat to the timeless traditions of Nokhur and the fiery depths of Darvaza. This was a land of contradictions—where Soviet relics stood alongside ancient beliefs, where presidential vanity projects met centuries-old customs, and where the starkness of the desert gave way to the lush valleys of the Kopet Dag mountains.

The people we met along the way had welcomed us with open hearts and endless plates of food, their hospitality a thread that connected every stop on our journey. From the intricate carpets of Nokhur to the roaring flames of the Darvaza Crater, Turkmenistan revealed itself as a land that refuses to fit neatly into any narrative.

The stars emerged once more, their light uninterrupted in the vast expanse of the desert sky, and I whispered to myself, "*This is why I travel—to find the rare in the ordinary, to uncover the stories hidden in the sands of time.*"

Chapter XII

SÃO TOMÉ AND PRÍNCIPE

December 2022

Adventure is worthwhile in itself.

– Amelia Earhart

There are places in this world that feel like secrets whispered by the wind, places that tug at your soul long before your feet touch their soil. São Tomé and Príncipe—two tiny islands adrift in the Gulf of Guinea—are just such a place. They beckon softly, not with grandiose promises or flashy attractions, but with the quiet allure of the unknown.

I wasn't traveling alone. Anand, was by my side—a rare occurrence given his preference for more historically-led destinations. As we settled into our seats on the small plane bound for São Tomé, I couldn't help but glance over at him. He was absorbed in a book, probably something historical, his way of grounding himself amidst the unfamiliar. This trip was as much his adventure as it was mine, and I could sense his curiosity quietly awakening.

Located off the western coast of Central Africa, São Tomé and Príncipe are Africa's second-smallest country and one of its most enigmatic. Their obscurity is part of their magic. Unlike the bustling beaches of Zanzibar or the iconic landscapes of the Serengeti, these islands remain a well-kept secret. Few travelers venture here, making it one of the least-visited countries in the world—a rare treasure in an era of overtourism.

As the plane began its descent, I nudged Anand and pointed out the window. His eyes widened as the emerald hills of São Tomé shimmered against the endless blue of the ocean. The larger of the two islands unfolded below us like a painting come to life, its volcanic peaks piercing through a dense canopy of rainforest. Beyond it lay Príncipe, its wilder sibling, cloaked in mist and mystery. The name São Tomé and Príncipe itself feels like poetry. It dances on the tongue, evoking images of rain-soaked jungles, golden beaches kissed by the Atlantic, and a culture that straddles continents. This wasn't just another destination. It felt like stepping into a story, one written in the salt air and red earth of the islands.

Before we left, our friends' reactions had been a mix of curiosity and skepticism.

"São Tomé and Príncipe? That sounds like a place you made up," one joked.

"It's real." I'd laughed, leaning into their bemusement with good humor. "And it's about to be unforgettable."

As we touched down, I sensed Anand's usual reservations about remote travel start to ease. The island welcomed us with its warm, humid air, rich with the mingling scents of salt, earth, and something sweet—perhaps cocoa or the intangible warmth of the tropics. The reality of the islands surpassed even my wildest imagination. São Tomé, with its sprawling cocoa plantations and colorful fishing villages, offered a vibrant tapestry of life. Here, history lingered in every corner, from the faded colonial facades to the stories carried by its people.

Príncipe was another world altogether—a haven where time seemed to have paused. Its dense rainforests, home to endemic bird species and rare orchids, pulsed with life. Pristine beaches stretched endlessly, their sands so untouched that my footprints felt like they might linger forever. I wasn't here for the usual—there were no towering skyscrapers, no throngs of tourists clamoring for the best selfie. Instead, these islands offered whispers of an untouched world: fishermen pulling in their nets at sunrise, markets alive with chatter and the scent of fresh spices, and rainforests echoing with the songs of birds found nowhere else on Earth. This was the kind of journey that transcended the superficial. São Tomé and Príncipe were not just islands; they were invitations. To listen. To learn. To see the world—and myself—with new eyes.

A Week in São Tomé and Príncipe

São Tomé... *A Symphony of Adventure*

Mornings in São Tomé began with a quiet enchantment. Sunlight streamed through the dense canopy surrounding our secluded villa, painting the wooden floors in a shifting mosaic of light and shadow. The air was rich with the mingling aromas of freshly brewed coffee and the yeasty warmth of bread straight from the oven—a siren call irresistible enough to draw us from the comfort of our slumber.

Fueled by a hearty breakfast, we set out to explore São Tomé's natural wonders. Our first destination was Obo Natural Park, a verdant sanctuary pulsating with life. The journey there was a visual feast, with the road meandering like a ribbon through a jungle so lush it seemed to pulse with its own heartbeat. Towering palms swayed in the breeze, their fronds casting dappled light on the forest floor below.

As the legendary Pico Cão Grande came into view, its jagged peak piercing the sky at an almost surreal 663 meters, a hush fell over us. The monolith rose like an ancient sentinel guarding the secrets of the forest, its summit veiled by wisps of mist that added an air of mystery. Climbing the trails that wrapped around the peak was like stepping into a primordial world. The forest was alive in every sense of the word: thick vines coiled around ancient trees, vibrant blooms peeked through the underbrush, and the air vibrated with birdsong. We paused often—not from exhaustion, but to absorb the sheer majesty of the landscape stretching endlessly before us. By late afternoon, we reached a vantage point just in time to watch the sun dip behind Pico Cão Grande. The sky erupted in hues of fiery orange, magenta, and violet, as if nature herself had saved her most stunning work for this moment. It was the kind of beauty that defies description—a fleeting masterpiece burned into memory.

Straddling the World's Edge at Praia Inhame

Twilight draped the sky in hues of lavender and rose as we reluctantly turned away from the fiery spectacle of Pico Cão Grande. The day's wonders had left us exhilarated, yet an air of anticipation hung thick as we made our way to Praia Inhame. The promise of island-hopping adventures lay ahead, and with it, the tantalizing allure of new discoveries waiting to unfold.

A small boat awaited us at the shore, its weathered hull rocking gently in rhythm with the tide. As we boarded, I couldn't help but feel like an explorer setting out into uncharted waters. The island we approached seemed to rise from the sea like a secret unveiled—a pristine paradise, untouched and enigmatic. Home to just 200 inhabitants, this secluded haven felt like a world apart from the bustling mainland.

The first sound to greet us was laughter. Joyous, unbridled, and pure, it came from a group of local children racing to the shore. Their bare feet slapped against the sand, kicking up tiny clouds that glowed golden in the fading light. Their smiles were as radiant as the tropical sun, their excitement contagious. It was as if our arrival was not just an event but a celebration, their laughter mingling with the rhythm of the waves to create a symphony of welcome. The beach itself was a marvel of wild beauty. Waves surged and crashed against ancient, weathered rocks, their timeless battle with the land etched into every curve and crevice. Just beyond, the water shifted to a serene expanse of crystalline blue, shimmering with an almost magical quality. The siren call of the ocean was irresistible, and before long, I found myself wading in. The water was cool and inviting, a refreshing contrast to the humid air that clung to my skin.

Standing at the shore, I was struck by an epiphany that sent a shiver down my spine. This wasn't just any beach; this was the equator. Right here, where the waves lapped at my feet, I stood astride the invisible line that divides our planet in two. The sheer enormity of that realization left me momentarily breathless. It wasn't just a geographical landmark—it was a symbol of connection, a reminder that the world, vast and varied as it may be, is intricately linked.

The journey back to our villa was bathed in the soft light of a retreating sun. Pico Cão Grande made one last appearance, its formidable silhouette standing proudly against a canvas of gold and violet. It felt like a silent farewell from the island's guardian, a reminder of the day's extraordinary experiences. As night fell, the villa came alive with the aromas of the sea. Fresh food, seasoned with local spices, teased my senses and set my stomach rumbling in anticipation. Each bite of our dinner was a revelation—a harmonious blend of flavors that captured the essence of São Tomé's vibrant culinary heritage.

I sat back, savoring the final taste of the meal,and my mind wandered over the day's wonders. São Tomé had already surpassed every expectation, its beauty and charm far richer than I could have imagined. And yet, as I gazed out at the starlit horizon, I knew this was only the beginning.

The island, with all its secrets and stories, was still waiting to reveal itself, one breathtaking moment at a time.

The Northern Reaches of São Tomé

The second day on São Tomé dawned in a watercolor dreamscape. Soft pinks and radiant golds bled across the horizon, the light spilling over the lush jungle and breathing life into every leaf and petal. The air was alive with a quiet anticipation, the kind that stirs the spirit and sharpens the senses.

As our vehicle rumbled to life and began its ascent along the winding northern roads, I found myself glued to the view outside. The road snaked through a labyrinth of emerald green, the dense foliage so thick it created its own microcosm. Vibrant tropical flowers—crimson, orange, and violet—bloomed like jewels hidden amidst the greenery, their colors heightened in the gentle light of dawn.

Above us, the sky peeked through the canopy in shards of azure, creating a hypnotic interplay of light and shadow. The forest seemed to breathe, each rustle of leaves and burst of birdsong amplifying the sense that we were passing through a realm where nature reigned supreme. The air was heavy with humidity, each inhalation laced with earthy petrichor, the sweet perfume of exotic blossoms, and the tangy zest of wild fruit ripening unseen in the undergrowth. The jungle held us in its embrace until we emerged into a quaint northern town. Here, history seemed to cling to every brick and stone.

Weathered colonial buildings lined the streets like elderly sentinels, their facades etched with time and wear. Cracks spider-webbed across their surfaces, softened by creeping vines and vibrant moss that nature had used to reclaim her space. Each structure whispered of bygone eras, their silent stories inviting us to pause and listen.

“Can you believe this place?” I whispered, my gaze drawn to an abandoned hospital. Its windows stared out like hollow eyes, their emptiness filled with the ghosts of lives once saved within its crumbling walls. It stood as a monument to São Tomé’s layered past—a place where echoes of colonial ambition and human resilience lingered in the air.

Yet, life in the town pulsed with an undeniable vibrancy, weaving itself around the remnants of history. Children darted between the buildings. Bare feet kicked up tiny clouds of ochre dust, which sparkled like fairy dust in the morning light.

One little girl broke from the group and approached us, her smile as bright and confident as the sun overhead.

“Olá!” she greeted us, her voice ringing out like a bell. Her name was Maria, she announced proudly, gesturing toward the other children peering shyly from behind a wall. They watched us with wide eyes, their curiosity a reminder of how we, too, must have seemed like peculiar visitors from another world. Kneeling to meet Maria’s gaze, I asked in my halting Portuguese, “Como você se chama?” She giggled, her joy so genuine it felt like it had filled the cracks of the old buildings around us. Her presence, along with the energy of the town's other children, was a poignant juxtaposition to the faded glory of the colonial structures. It was as if the resilience of São Tomé's people breathed new life into the history that surrounded them.

As we wandered deeper into the streets, the air seemed to thrum with memories. The resonant tones of ancient church bells called out, their melancholic melody weaving through the fabric of the town. They seemed to summon not just the devout but also the stories of a complex and layered past. Adding to this sensory tapestry was the aroma of freshly baked bread wafting from a nearby bakery. It was impossible not to follow the scent, which seemed to pull us forward like an invisible thread. Inside, the baker worked with practiced precision, the golden loaves emerging from the oven an ode to a craft that had weathered the island's changing tides.

The cobblestones beneath our feet were worn smooth from centuries of passage, their surface holding the weight of countless stories. Faded murals peeked through tangles of bougainvillea, their vibrant colors partially obscured but still defiant in their beauty. These painted scenes told tales of São Tomé's colonial past, its cultural identity, and the enduring spirit of its people. Here was a place where history didn't fade away—it adapted, intertwined with the present to create something both poignant and alive.

By the time we returned to our vehicle, I was filled with a quiet reverence for the journey we had taken.

The northern reaches of São Tomé had revealed themselves to be more than a destination—they were a reflection of life itself: layered, imperfect, and undeniably beautiful.

Príncipe: A Wild Eden

If São Tomé is a lush symphony, Príncipe is its untamed encore. The smaller of the two islands, it welcomed us with an explosion of greenery and an undeniable sense of stepping into another time. The journey northward took us through undulating hills blanketed in coffee plantations, their earthy aroma hanging thick in the air.

Lagoa Azul, the Blue Lagoon, was our first stop. Cresting a hill, we were greeted by a view so exquisite it took our breath away. The lagoon shimmered like a sheet of polished sapphire, its vibrant hues contrasting with the verdant green of the surrounding forest. Collective gasps echoed in the silence. There it was, stretching out like a liquid jewel—a vast sheet of polished sapphire shimmering under the sun's caress. Ripples sent diamonds of light skittering across its surface, while glistening white sands bordered the lagoon like a halo, glowing with an inner radiance. The lagoon's tranquility was mirrored by the lush green forest that hugged its edges, a contrast so striking it felt almost surreal.

"Shall we snorkel?" I asked, already entranced by the crystalline waters. The mere thought of diving into that serene world sent a thrill of excitement through me. The moment we slipped beneath the surface, it was as though we had entered another realm entirely. The lagoon transformed into an underwater paradise, alive with movement and color. Schools of tropical fish, their scales shimmering like living gemstones, darted around us with a synchronized grace. Coral formations in hues of amber, lavender, and emerald rose like underwater cathedrals, intricate and timeless.

Each breath through my snorkel was a reminder of how foreign I was to this aquatic kingdom, the sound of my presence contrasting with the muted symphony of life all around me. Time seemed to dissolve, replaced by the simple wonder of coexistence with creatures who moved with the effortless elegance of nature itself. Reluctantly, we emerged from the lagoon's embrace, its magic still clinging to our senses. The journey continued, taking us through undulating hills swathed in coffee plantations that stretched endlessly into the horizon.

The Art of Coffee and a Botanical Paradise

We arrived at one of São Tomé's renowned coffee farms, where the legacy of coffee-making was alive and thriving. Entering the processing area felt like stepping into a living tradition. Women moved with a precision that was both practical and poetic, their hands flying over piles of beans as they sorted them with unerring expertise.

The rhythmic sound of beans being sifted, combined with the occasional murmur of conversation, created an almost meditative atmosphere. Each bean was a story, a labor of love that linked generations of farmers to the land. Watching them work wasn't just an education—it was an immersion into a way of life, a connection to something enduring and deeply rooted in the island's identity.

The road then carried us to a botanical garden that felt like a scene from a dream. Towering begonias stretched skyward, their blooms the size of dinner plates, radiating colors so vibrant they seemed to pulse with energy. Orchids peeked shyly from shaded corners, their delicate petals shimmering like mother-of-pearl in the dappled sunlight. "This place is unreal," I murmured, trailing my fingers along the velvety edge of a flower as wide as my hand. Each step brought a new marvel: leaves etched with patterns that looked painted by an artist, petals so vivid they seemed to defy nature.

Towering trees with massive trunks created a cathedral-like canopy, their branches weaving an intricate lattice above us. The air was heavy with the mingling fragrances of flowers, soil, and the faintest trace of rain. Every so often, a rustle in the underbrush or a burst of color in the canopy hinted at the diverse wildlife that called this paradise home, adding an element of surprise to the serenity.

Cascata São Nicolau

As the day began to wane, we made our way to Cascata São Nicolau, São Tomé's renowned waterfall. Its voice reached us long before its form—a low, resonant roar that seemed to vibrate through the ground and into our bones.

When the trail turned its final corner, the waterfall came into view. Sheets of water plunged down a sheer rock face with unrelenting force, their movement transforming the air into a fine mist that cooled our sun-warmed skin. The afternoon light struck the spray, creating a shimmering golden veil that danced with the waterfall's rhythm. Standing there, I felt the power of nature in its purest form—a force that both humbled and uplifted. The roar of the water drowned out every other sound, commanding attention and quieting the mind.

São Tomé was a living, breathing entity, a place that demanded more than observation. It called for immersion—for travelers to step into its rhythm, to listen to its stories, and to leave a piece of their hearts behind. Even as twilight wrapped the island in its embrace, the siren call of São Tomé lingered in my mind. There was still so much to uncover, so many mysteries waiting to be unraveled. Each revelation deepened my connection to the island, promising that even if one stayed a lifetime, there would always be another secret to discover, another breathtaking vista to marvel at.

Closing Thoughts

As the cascade thundered before me, mist rising in delicate swirls that danced with the sunlight, I felt a deep stillness settle in my chest—a rare moment where beauty silences all else. São Tomé and Príncipe are like that. They whisper, rather than shout, offering quiet revelations rather than overwhelming spectacles.

These islands, cradled in the azure embrace of the Gulf of Guinea are a living paradox. For all their natural splendor carries the weight of survival in an unpredictable world. The global market, fickle as the tides, has left the islands' traditional lifelines, like coffee and cocoa, teetering on the edge of uncertainty. Yet São Tomé and Príncipe endure, like their volcanic peaks that rise against all odds.

"In 2017, France welcomed over 87 million visitors," I mused, my voice soft against the symphony of water. "And São Tomé and Príncipe? Just 25,000." My husband's raised eyebrows mirrored my own disbelief when I first read that statistic. To think that such untouched beauty remained largely undiscovered in a world overflowing with tourism was staggering.

"Imagine," I continued, gesturing to the primordial landscape enveloping us, "having an entire island to yourself. It's a kind of magic that feels almost impossible these days."

As we began our descent from the waterfall, the path revealed new vistas with each turn—ferns unfurling in the damp shade, sunbeams filtering through the canopy like nature's spotlight. The trail mirrored what São Tomé and Príncipe represent: the thrill of discovery at every step, a journey into the unknown where every clearing holds the promise of something extraordinary.

"What draws me to places like this," I confessed as the golden light of late afternoon bathed the forest, "is the mystery. You're not just visiting—you're peeling back layers. Every path leads to something untouched, something few have seen. It's the ultimate freedom."

Freedom was the thread that wove through this journey: freedom from crowds, from schedules, from the noise of the world. On these islands, the unpredictable weather seemed like a playful nudge, reminding us to embrace the present. Plans shifted with the rhythm of the tides and the whims of the sky, and somehow, that was perfect.

"Flexibility isn't just a virtue here," I said with a chuckle. "It's a survival skill. But isn't that the joy of it? Letting go of control and just... being." The essence of São Tomé and Príncipe lies in that surrender—in trading rigid itineraries for the unhurried pulse of island life. It's in hopping from one secluded beach to another, each a masterpiece more stunning than the last. It's in wandering jungles so untouched that your footprints might be the first in days. And it's in connecting with a way of life that slows your heartbeat and sharpens your senses.

As the day drew to a close and the waterfall's roar faded behind us, I felt the weight of being a traveler here—a responsibility as profound as it was thrilling. Each meal we savored, each piece of art we purchased, each guided trek we took contributed to the delicate balance of sustaining this fragile paradise. "These islands don't just need visitors," I said as the sky shifted to twilight, hues of violet and amber spreading like an artist's brushstroke. "They need stewards—people who come not to take, but to witness, to honor, and to protect." Standing there, with the jungle's nocturnal hum rising around me and the last rays of sunlight painting the horizon, I realized São Tomé and Príncipe had done more than reveal their beauty. They had reminded me of why I travel: to bear witness to the stories of our world, to connect with the raw and unfiltered essence of life, and to leave each place with the knowledge that I, too, am part of its narrative.

These islands, with their mist-shrouded peaks and palm-fringed shores, are more than just a destination for the adventurous. They are a call to rediscover the essence of travel itself—the joy of stepping into the unknown, the wonder of finding humanity in its purest forms, and the humility of knowing that every footprint matters. So, to the dreamers, the wanderers, and the curious souls who long for more than just another destination on a map, I extend this invitation: go to São Tomé and Príncipe. Let their unspoiled beauty awaken your spirit. Walk the paths where few have tread, breathe in the air rich with stories, and lose yourself in the timeless rhythm of their shores. For in São Tomé and Príncipe, every dawn carries the promise of a new discovery, and every moment spent is a reminder that the rarest treasures are those found in places that speak to the soul. The islands await, their secrets waiting to be uncovered, their beauty unmatched. Will you answer their call?

Chapter XIII

COMOROS

December 2022

> ***In every out-of-the-way place, there is a piece of yourself waiting to be found.***
>
> ***– Jhumpa Lahiri***

Comoros isn't the kind of destination that announces itself. It doesn't shout from glossy travel brochures or flood social media feeds with bucket-list hashtags. Instead, it's a quiet whisper, the kind that lingers in the air long after you've first heard it. It's the soft pull of curiosity that led me here, to an archipelago strung across the Indian Ocean like an unfinished thought—waiting, perhaps, for someone to complete its story. The islands welcomed us with a breeze that carried an intoxicating mix of sea salt, ylang-ylang blossoms, and volcanic earth. The sun, still heavy with the promises of late afternoon, bathed everything in hues of honey and amber, making the palm trees seem like they were glowing from within.

"Do you think anyone will believe us when we tell them where we are?" I asked Anand as we stood on the tarmac, the warmth of the island already wrapping itself around us. He grinned, equal parts amused and bewildered. "Probably not. But that's what makes it perfect."

It was true. Comoros wasn't the kind of place that fit neatly into conversations back home. Most of our friends hadn't even heard of it. And that's what made standing here so exhilarating—it felt like stepping into the unknown, into a chapter that hadn't yet been written. Somewhere between Madagascar and Mozambique, Comoros lies suspended in a corner of the world few ever think to explore. Four islands form the archipelago: Ngazidja (Grande Comore), dominated by the imposing silhouette of Mount Karthala; Ndzuwani (Anjouan), with its jagged peaks and scented plantations; Mwali (Mohéli), a sanctuary of untouched marine life; and Mayotte, where French influence mingles with the islands' natural beauty.

Each island has a rhythm, a soul of its own. And as we stepped into this realm, it felt as though the air itself was whispering secrets of what was to come—secluded beaches, rainforests alive with unknown sounds, and a culture that didn't demand to be understood, only experienced.

The world had 197 countries, 8 billion people, and infinite places to visit. Yet here we were, standing in one of the least-visited nations on Earth. The enormity of it hit me then, not as a boast, but as a quiet realization. This trip wasn't about finding Comoros on a map—it was about finding something within myself in a place that seemed, by design, to exist outside the noise.

And maybe that's what Comoros really is: a whisper. One you only hear if you're willing to stop and listen.

"Can you believe this place has only seen about 20,000 visitors a year?" Anand mused with a voice tinged with disbelief and wonder. The number hung between us, suspended in the air as though it carried its own weight, its very existence a testament to how little known this land truly was. I turned my gaze toward the horizon, where the cerulean waters kissed the powder-white sands in an effortless, eternal embrace. "Imagine," I whispered, my words almost lost to the gentle rhythm of the waves, "what lies beyond those shores."

A shiver of anticipation ran through me at the thought. Here, on these islands, there would be no competing for space, no crowded beaches, no tourist traps to navigate. Just the thought of having entire stretches of coastline to ourselves, or stumbling upon a waterfall hidden deep within the jungle, untouched and waiting for someone to claim it, sent a thrill through my chest.

But Comoros was not just a place for the lonely wanderer. Its allure wasn't solely in its untouched natural beauty. It was something far deeper, something more elusive. It was in the pulse of the land, the stories woven into its culture, a heady blend of African, Arab, and French influences that blended into something entirely unique. The islands whispered stories of ancient sultans who had once ruled over prosperous kingdoms, their legacies alive in the walls of forgotten medinas, in the rhythms of traditional Comorian music that seemed to vibrate with centuries of history.

The warmth of the island wrapped itself around us like a long-lost embrace when we stepped into the modest airport terminal. Local smiles greeted us as though we were not strangers but welcome guests, familiar faces in a place untouched by the chaos of the modern world. The people of Comoros carried in their eyes stories of resilience. They had withstood political upheavals, natural calamities, and the challenges of isolation, yet their spirit remained—radiating warmth, generosity, and an unspoken understanding of how to live with what the earth and the sea offered.

This, I reminded myself, was why I traveled. To seek out places like Comoros, where stories were not told in a rush, where treasures were not on display for the masses but hidden in corners of the world still unknown to the ordinary traveler. To step into a space where I could challenge my own perceptions and see the world in its raw, unrefined beauty. Comoros was not merely a place on the map; it was an invitation. An invitation to turn away from the ordinary, to reject the predictable, and instead embrace the mysteries that only the truly off-the-beaten-path destinations could offer. With its volcanic peaks shrouded in mist, its lagoons brimming with marine life, and the air thick with the scent of tropical blooms, Comoros was a land where every moment felt like an enigma waiting to be unveiled.

We picked up our bags and stepped out into the sunshine, and I knew one thing for certain: This journey would be one to remember. It wouldn't just be about exploring an unknown place—it would be about creating a story, a tale of wonder and discovery that would unfold with every step we took, every path we ventured down, and every piece of this extraordinary world we uncovered. The unknown was calling, and we were ready to answer.

Moheli Island

The boat hummed softly as it carved through the glassy expanse of the Indian Ocean, Moheli rising before us like a secret waiting to be uncovered. The smallest of the Comoros islands, it seemed almost shy, its emerald cliffs veiled in mist and fringed by beaches that shimmered like powdered gold. The closer we drew, the more it felt like we were approaching a world untouched—a refuge far from the noise of everywhere else.

The pier jutted out over water so clear it felt unreal, each wave brushing against the wood with a whisper. As we disembarked, the air smelled of salt and frangipani, a heady mix that seemed to welcome us into the island's fold. Laka Lodge, a cluster of colorful cottages nestled among swaying palms, peeked out from behind a jungle of green, its coral, turquoise, and sunflower hues a cheerful contrast to the natural world around it.

"This place," Anand said, looking around in awe, "feels like it knows secrets we're not supposed to find out all at once."

I laughed but couldn't shake the same feeling. Moheli was the kind of place that made you curious about what lay beyond every curve of its coastline or deep within its forests. Even standing still felt like being on the brink of discovery. Within an hour, the ocean had pulled us in. The water was warm, a liquid embrace that felt like it belonged to a different time—an age before the world grew busy. Slipping on our snorkels, we dove into what seemed like another universe. Below the surface, the reef stretched like a sprawling city, alive with motion. Corals, shaped like brains, fans, and abstract sculptures, swayed in the currents, creating homes for a kaleidoscope of marine life. Tiny, electric-blue fish flitted between the branches, while larger ones—striped and spotted like miniature works of art—hovered near coral caves.

And then, the turtles.

I froze as the first one came into view, its silhouette graceful and ancient, as though it carried millennia of stories within its shell. Its flippers moved with an elegance that seemed to defy physics, gliding effortlessly through the water. Another appeared, and then a third, their movements synchronized like a slow, meditative dance. "They're everywhere!" I gestured wildly to Anand, my excitement muffled by the snorkel. He nodded, his eyes wide, pointing to one floating just beneath us, nibbling on a patch of sea grass. It was surreal, watching something so prehistoric move with such calm in a world that often felt anything but.

Hours slipped by as we swam among them, the sun dipping lower until the water turned a deep shade of gold. Emerging from the ocean, we collapsed on the beach, our skin tingling from salt and sun, and watched the sky shift into a symphony of colors—pink blending into orange, orange dissolving into indigo.

The day had been full of discoveries, but it wasn't just the sights that stayed with me. It was the quiet intimacy of the island, the way it offered itself not as a destination to conquer but as a place to simply be. As the first stars began to emerge above us, I felt a strange sense of belonging here, on this tiny island that seemed to exist outside time. And though I didn't yet know all its secrets, I couldn't wait to find out what else it had in store.

Moheli National Park

The Hope for the Livingstone Fruit Bats

The day began with a promise in the air, carried on the golden glow of the island's sunrise. We laced up our hiking boots, ready to venture deep into the heart of Moheli National Park. It wasn't just a hike—it was a mission to encounter one of the island's most extraordinary residents: the Livingstone Fruit Bat. The trail pulled us into the forest almost immediately, the outside world disappearing behind a curtain of green. The air was thick with humidity, alive with the scent of earth and leaves. Droplets of dew clung to the edges of vines and fronds, shimmering in the early light. Around us, the symphony of the jungle played on—chirping insects, rustling leaves, and the occasional call of an unseen bird.

"This is a workout," Anand joked, wiping his forehead as the trail steepened. He wasn't wrong—each step was a small triumph as we ascended through tangled roots and moss-covered stones. But the promise of seeing these rare, otherworldly bats spurred us onward. An hour into the climb, we reached a clearing where a team of researchers was waiting. Dressed in rugged field gear, they greeted us warmly, their enthusiasm for their work palpable. "Welcome to the Livingstone Fruit Bat's domain," one of them said, gesturing to the towering trees that surrounded us.

The bats, they explained, are not your average flying mammals. "These are the sky's gentle giants," one biologist said, her eyes lighting up. "They're among the largest bats in the world, with wingspans that can reach an astonishing 1.5 meters." She held her arms wide for emphasis, and the sheer scale was hard to fathom.

"But they're not just big," she continued. "They're also vital. These bats are critical pollinators and seed dispersers, helping to maintain the health of this entire forest." Without them, many of the fruit trees and plants we admired might struggle to survive.

Another researcher chimed in with a surprising fact: unlike their insect-eating cousins, fruit bats rely on a diet of figs, guavas, and other tropical fruits. "They've got sharp teeth for tearing into fruit and tongues designed to lap up nectar," she explained. "Think of them as nature's gardeners, planting trees wherever they fly."

What made the Livingstone Fruit Bats even more fascinating was their rarity. "They're only found here in the Comoros," the lead biologist said with concern. "There are fewer than 1,200 left in the wild. Habitat loss is the biggest threat." It was sobering to realize that this creature, so integral to the ecosystem, was teetering on the brink of extinction. Our conversation was interrupted by a soft rustling above. The researchers exchanged knowing glances, their movements quiet and deliberate as they pointed to the canopy. "There," one of them whispered.

We craned our necks, eyes scanning the treetops, and then—a massive shape emerged from the shadows. A Livingstone Fruit Bat soared into view, its leathery wings stretched wide against the sunlight. The sheer size of it was breathtaking. Its fur, a burnished golden brown, glowed faintly in the dappled light as it glided effortlessly through the trees. "They use those wings like a parachute," the biologist whispered. "Each flap is energy-efficient, perfect for long-distance flying. And those sharp claws? They can hang upside down for hours without breaking a sweat." The bat paused on a high branch, its head tilting slightly as though surveying its surroundings. Even from a distance, its large, soulful eyes were striking—adapted not for echo-location like other bats, but for seeing clearly in low light. It was as if the creature had been built for a life of quiet grace.

Watching it felt like stepping into another world. For a brief moment, we were no longer visitors but participants in the ancient rhythm of the forest. As the bat launched itself back into the sky and disappeared among the trees, the spell broke. I realized I had been holding my breath, caught between awe and gratitude for the chance to witness something so rare and extraordinary. The trek back to Laka Lodge was filled with hushed conversation. Every crackle of leaves or shift in the breeze felt like a continuation of the magic we'd just experienced. Moheli wasn't just a beautiful island—it was a sanctuary, a reminder of the fragile balance that keeps places like this alive.

The Livingstone Fruit Bat was more than just a symbol of Moheli's uniqueness. It was a testament to the interconnectedness of life, a quiet guardian of a forest that depended on it as much as we depended on the air we breathed.

Witnessing Giant Turtles Lay Eggs

The excitement of the day lingered long into the evening as we prepared for one of nature's most profound spectacles—a midnight excursion to Itsamia Beach to witness giant turtles laying their eggs. Even as the sun dipped below the horizon, anticipation buzzed through the air at Laka Lodge.

"Ready for an unforgettable night?" Anand asked, his grin wide. I nodded, already imagining what lay ahead. We set off under a sky so densely packed with stars it seemed like a celestial mosaic, the Milky Way stretching out in all its brilliance. The night hummed with life—the rhythmic crash of distant waves, the persistent chatter of insects, and the occasional rustle of unseen creatures. It felt as if the world was holding its breath, waiting for what was to come. Itsamia Beach, we soon learned, is not just any nesting site.

It's a critical haven for green sea turtles, which are the largest of the hard-shelled turtle species. Here, hundreds of females come ashore annually, continuing a journey that has been repeated for over 100 million years—making turtles one of the oldest creatures on Earth.

Upon reaching the beach, we were greeted by a conservationist who shared guidelines for minimizing our impact. "These turtles have traveled thousands of kilometers across the Indian Ocean to lay their eggs here," she said, her tone reverent. "Some of them even return to the same beach where they were born, guided by the Earth's magnetic field." The idea that these turtles navigated vast oceans to this precise location was mind-boggling.

The waiting began. Time slipped by in an oddly comforting rhythm—eyes scanning the shoreline, ears tuned to the soft whispers of waves. Suddenly, a volunteer whispered, "There she is." We turned to see a massive green sea turtle emerging from the waves, her silhouette illuminated by the moonlight. At over 150 kilograms, she seemed like a creature from another age, her glistening shell a testament to the ocean's resilience. Watching her laboriously drag herself up the sand was humbling; every movement seemed purposeful, almost sacred.

When she began digging, the conservationist beside me whispered fascinating details. Using her hind flippers like shovels, she carved a perfect nest deep in the sand, ensuring the eggs would remain protected from predators and temperature extremes. "She can lay between 100 and

200 eggs," the volunteer said. "And the sand's temperature determines the hatchlings' sex—cooler sand produces males, while warmer sand yields females."

As the turtle began depositing her eggs, I felt an overwhelming sense of privilege. Here was an ancient ritual—an unbroken chain of life stretching back millions of years. Once she finished, she carefully covered the nest, ensuring the eggs were hidden from view. Then, with a deliberate slowness, she made her way back to the sea, leaving only faint tracks behind.

The entire experience felt timeless. As she disappeared into the waves, I thought about how fewer and fewer turtles make this journey each year, their survival threatened by habitat loss, plastic pollution, and climate change. Yet, in her silent persistence, there was hope—a reminder of nature's resilience and the delicate balance we must protect.

Feeding Lemurs

After the late-night adventure on Itsamia Beach, we allowed ourselves the luxury of a lazy morning at Laka Lodge. But nature had other plans to keep us entertained. As we sipped our morning coffee on the veranda, a rustling in the nearby trees caught my eye.

"Lemurs!" I exclaimed, leaping to my feet.

There they were, their long, bushy tails dangling like streamers from the branches. These charismatic primates moved with a mix of grace and mischief, their black-and-white fur contrasting vividly against the green canopy.

Although lemurs are native to Madagascar, the Comoros Islands are home to introduced populations of mongoose lemurs and brown lemurs. These species were brought over centuries ago, likely by sailors or traders, and have since adapted to the islands' unique ecosystems.

"They have their own little society," Anand remarked as we watched one lemur gently groom another. Lemurs are known for their complex social structures, living in matriarchal groups where females typically call the shots—a rare arrangement in the animal kingdom.

I couldn't resist the urge to interact. Grabbing a bunch of bananas I'd purchased at a local market, I approached cautiously, holding out a piece of fruit. A particularly bold lemur crept forward, his round, amber eyes locking onto mine. He reached out with his tiny, leathery hand, snatched the banana, and scurried back to safety.

The moment his fingers brushed mine, I felt an odd thrill. It wasn't just their physicality but the intelligence behind their eyes—a glimpse into a world parallel to our own. Lemurs, as I later learned, are highly intelligent, capable of problem-solving and even forming bonds with humans in environments where they feel safe.

Soon, more lemurs joined the fray. Their antics were endlessly entertaining—from acrobatic leaps between branches to the way they clutched bananas like toddlers with candy. Watching them so up-close revealed details I hadn't noticed before: their soft, fur-lined ears twitching at every sound, their long tails curling like question marks as they balanced on thin branches. One lemur paused to lick its hand, spreading the scent of its saliva onto the bark of a tree. "That's how they mark their territory," Anand observed. Lemurs use scent glands on their wrists and tails to communicate with one another, leaving messages of dominance, mating status, or even friendship.

The unexpected encounter added a playful dimension to the day. Against the backdrop of Moheli's lush landscapes, feeding these lively primates felt like sharing a moment with the wild—a reminder that even in remote corners of the world, life thrives in its own beautiful, unpredictable ways.

Grand Comore

As much as Moheli had charmed us with its untamed beauty, it was time to continue our Comorian adventure. With hearts brimming with memories and camera rolls overflowing with snapshots of sunsets, turtles, and mischievous lemurs, we reluctantly bid farewell to Laka Lodge and boarded a boat bound for Grand Comore.

Approaching Moroni, the capital city, felt like stepping into a different world. While Moheli had been a sanctuary of untouched wilderness, Moroni thrummed with a quiet yet vibrant energy. The city spread out before us, a labyrinth of narrow streets flanked by buildings adorned with intricately carved wooden doors and coral-stone walls. Each corner seemed to whisper stories of the island's Swahili-Arabic heritage.

The air carried a distinct aroma—a heady blend of salty sea breeze, the warm spice of clove and cinnamon markets, and the intoxicating floral scent of ylang-ylang blossoms. Comoros is one of the world's leading producers of ylang-ylang oil, a key ingredient in high-end perfumes like Chanel No. 5. Walking through Moroni, it felt as though the essence of the island was woven into the very air we breathed.

It became clear that Moroni's charm lay in its contrasts. Fishing boats bobbed gently in the harbor while women in vibrantly patterned kangas carried baskets of fruit atop their heads. The city seemed to operate at its own pace, unhurried yet full of purpose. That evening, our guide introduced us to the next chapter of our adventure: a hike up Mount Karthala. "It's the largest active volcano in the Indian Ocean," he explained, with excitement in his eyes. The idea of trekking to the summit of such a monumental force of nature sent a jolt of anticipation through me.

Karthala Volcano

The morning of the hike arrived with a clear, sapphire sky. Mount Karthala loomed on the horizon, its rugged silhouette dominating the island's landscape. At over 2,360 meters, this active shield volcano is both a geological marvel and a vital part of Comoros' identity. It's erupted more than 20 times since the 19th century, and its most recent eruption in 2005 left ash deposits that temporarily displaced thousands.

We began our ascent, the path winding through an ecosystem that seemed to evolve with every step. At the base, lush tropical vegetation enveloped us, the air thick with the earthy scent of damp soil and flowering hibiscus. Here, we encountered endemic birds like the Karthala scops owl, a species found nowhere else in the world. Its haunting call echoed through the trees, a reminder of the biodiversity nurtured by this volcanic island. On climbing higher, the forest thinned and gave way to an otherworldly terrain of jagged volcanic rock and windswept plateaus. The contrast was stark, the greenery below replaced by barren expanses shaped by ancient lava flows. The trail demanded focus and endurance, but the views were worth every step. From this vantage point, the island unfolded like a living map—the verdant hills, sparkling coastline, and the vast expanse of the Indian Ocean stretching endlessly into the horizon.

Reaching the summit felt like stepping onto another planet. The crater, a yawning expanse of black rock and steaming fissures, exuded an almost primal energy. Peering into its depths, I could see molten lava churning like a furious cauldron. The red-orange glow illuminated the surrounding darkness, while tendrils of smoke spiraled upward, carrying with them the sulfurous scent of the Earth's core. Karthala's crater is enormous, stretching over 3 kilometers wide, and its sheer size is humbling. Shield volcanoes like Karthala are known for their gentle slopes and expansive craters, a stark contrast to the steep, cone-shaped stratovolcanoes like Mount Fuji. Yet, their eruptions can be equally dramatic, as the volcano slowly but powerfully expels molten rock from its depths.

Standing at the edge of the crater, I couldn't help but marvel at the immense forces at play beneath our feet. It was both terrifying and awe-inspiring—a visceral reminder of the Earth's power to create and destroy. The volcano isn't just a geological wonder; it's also a vital part of Comorian life. The fertile soils created by ancient eruptions support the island's agriculture, including the ylang-ylang and vanilla plantations that define its economy.

As we began our descent, the sun dipped toward the horizon, casting long shadows across the rugged landscape. I carried the memory of the bubbling lava and the heat radiating from the Earth's depths like a talisman—a reminder of the raw, untamed beauty of this island and the planet we call home.

Lac Sale Exploration

Our final day in Comoros dawned with a bittersweet edge. The thrill of one last adventure mingled with the weight of knowing our time in this magical archipelago was coming to an end. But Comoros, it seemed, had saved one of its most enigmatic wonders for last: Lac Sale, a volcanic crater lake whispered about in local legends and celebrated for its mesmerizing, ever-changing hues. The trail meandered through patches of dense greenery, and every so often, a breeze carried faint echoes of birdsong and the distant rustle of leaves. Our guide shared stories about Lac Sale's reputation among locals—a place believed to hold secrets beneath its shimmering surface.

"Legend says two divers disappeared here," I mentioned, recalling tales I'd read about the lake.

"Some say they were cursed, others believe it's the lake's unfathomable depth that swallowed them whole." The thought sent a shiver through me, the lake's mythical aura amplifying the suspense, taking me back to my childhood in an instance. As a child, my evenings often unfolded into epics, with my Thatha—my paternal grandfather—guiding me through the labyrinth of myth and heroism. After dinner, we would sit together in the soft glow of the night, and he would open the pages of the Mahabharata. Each chapter felt like a revelation, filled with larger-than-life warriors, divine interventions, and moral dilemmas. I wasn't just listening; I was living those battles, marching alongside Arjuna, deciphering Krishna's enigmatic wisdom, and grappling with Draupadi's resilience. Those stories planted the seeds of a deep-rooted fascination with the wild, the fierce, and the boundless potential of human courage. Even now, as I journey through the farthest corners of the world, that little girl—entranced by tales of valor and vengeance—still lingers within me. She surfaced again in Comoros, as I listened to the local legends that wove through the islands like an invisible thread. The tale of Lac Salé, cursed and mysterious, transported me back to my childhood, where snakes became protectors of my family, bound by a mythical pact forged generations ago. It reminded me of the Tamil folklore of Ali Arasan, the heroic king who carved his fate against all odds, or the sweeping saga of Ponniyin Selvan, a story where destiny and bravery collide with unrelenting force.

These myths, whether born in the Indian subcontinent or the heart of Africa, share a kinship. They arise from humanity's attempt to explain the inexplicable, to transform chaos into a narrative that feels tangible. But for me, they're more than just tales. They are reminders of the untamed spirit that lies within us all—a call to embrace the unknown, to seek out stories that challenge the mundane and ignite the extraordinary.

Perhaps that's why I've always been drawn to the wild and the heroic. Comoros, with its untamed landscapes and whispered legends, felt like stepping into a living epic. The volcanic craters, the scent of ylang-ylang in the air, and the rhythmic pulse of the Indian Ocean—all of it carried a fierceness that mirrored the tales of old. It was as though the islands themselves were characters in their own mythology, daring you to uncover their secrets. Listening to the elders recount their stories in Comoros, I found myself doing what I've done all my life—drawing parallels, connecting dots, finding the familiar in the foreign. My love for myths is as much about what they reveal about a culture as it is about what they reveal about ourselves. The fables of cursed lakes, vengeful spirits, and heroic deeds are a shared language, transcending borders and reminding us of the fierceness and fragility of being human.

But all notions of curses and mystery evaporated the moment we laid eyes on Lac Sale. It was as if we had stumbled upon an illusion crafted by nature herself. The water seemed alive, shifting colors like a mood ring. Deep emeralds dissolved into sapphire blues, only to morph into vibrant turquoise as the sunlight and clouds played their eternal dance overhead. It felt almost supernatural, as if the lake were a portal to another world. We walked its perimeter, stopping frequently to marvel at how the colors transformed with every step. At times, it resembled a gemstone glinting in the sun; at others, a vast inkblot, dark and impenetrable. The crater's steep, jagged walls framed the lake like a fortress, their shadows adding to the mystique. Surrounding the lake, wild vegetation clung to the volcanic soil, its vivid green hues contrasting starkly with the mineral-rich waters.

Beyond its beauty, Lac Sale carries cultural and ecological significance. The volcanic forces that created it continue to shape the lives of Comorians, from the fertile soils that sustain their agriculture to the geothermal activity that powers their myths and traditions. Even its name, "Salt Lake," hints at its volcanic origins, as the water is said to hold a high mineral content, giving it a strange buoyancy. As the afternoon wore on, we hiked to a nearby viewpoint that offered a breathtaking panorama. From here, Lac Sale glistened like a jewel embedded in the Earth, while the ocean stretched endlessly in the distance. The view seemed to capture the spirit of Comoros itself—a seamless blend of raw, volcanic intensity and serene, oceanic beauty. Standing there, I reflected on everything these islands had revealed. From Moheli's secluded beaches teeming with marine life to Grand Comore's rugged volcanic landscapes, every moment had been a testament to the archipelago's diversity. Lac Sale, with its hypnotic colors and legends, felt like a perfect ending—an emblem of Comoros' ability to surprise and captivate.

As the sun dipped low, the lake mirrored the sky's kaleidoscope of colors—gold melting into amber, then deepening into crimson and violet. It was a final performance, a grand farewell orchestrated by nature itself. I felt a deep sense of gratitude: for the beauty we had been privileged to witness, for the unassuming magic of this archipelago, and for the people whose warmth and hospitality had turned us from visitors into admirers.

Comoros, I realized, was not merely a tropical destination. It was a symphony of contrasts—where fiery volcanoes coexisted with tranquil beaches, and legends intertwined with breathtaking reality. As we made our way back to our lodgings for the last time, I found myself already dreaming of a return

Final Thoughts

The sun blazed over Comoros, casting glittering reflections across the Indian Ocean, but the islands' serenity masked their deeper struggles. Political turbulence and economic uncertainty are ever-present, shaping daily life in ways a casual visitor might miss. And yet, standing on these volcanic shores, I couldn't help but marvel at a paradox: a place so unassuming, yet so profoundly stirring.

Adventure here isn't about curated itineraries or postcard-perfect luxury; it's about raw, unscripted encounters. Comoros doesn't seduce you with grandeur—it challenges you to look closer, to understand. And for those who accept, the rewards are incomparable. One morning, I watched a fisherman tug his wooden canoe ashore, his hands rough from years of labor but precise as he untangled his nets. Behind him, ylang-ylang trees swayed in the breeze, their blossoms perfuming the air with a sweetness that lingered long after. In that moment, Comoros revealed its essence: a life shaped by nature, resilience, and quiet dignity.

This isn't the kind of destination that hands you easy thrills. Hiking to Karthala's smoldering crater requires effort; wading into the waters of Moheli to glimpse dolphins demands patience. But when the rewards come—a volcanic sunrise painting the horizon in fiery hues, a lemur gripping your hand like an old friend—they're unforgettable. For those drawn to Comoros, practicality is key. Luxury resorts are absent, replaced by simple lodges and local homestays. The island's markets—chaotic, colorful, and bursting with life—offer a glimpse into its soul. Here, vendors call out their goods, the scents of freshly caught fish mingling with ripe fruit and handmade crafts. There's a rhythm to it, an unhurried pace that's oddly soothing.

Travel here isn't just an escape; it's an immersion. Each interaction, whether a shared meal of fragrant pilau or a casual chat with a guide, feels authentic, unvarnished. These aren't experiences designed to impress tourists; they're glimpses into a culture still rooted in its traditions, even as it contends with modern challenges. On one of my last evenings, I found myself alone on a crescent beach, the sand cool underfoot, waves lapping at the shore. Overhead, the sky was an expanse of stars so brilliant it felt as though they might tumble into the ocean. Nearby, a giant sea turtle labored ashore, instinct guiding her to bury her eggs in the sand.

If you come here, come with curiosity. Choose local guides who know the land's stories and traditions. Wander the markets, taste the food, and ask questions. Support the people who keep this place alive—not just for their sake, but because their insights will enrich your journey. As I prepared to leave, the thought of returning felt inevitable. Comoros had a way of getting under my skin, with its volcanic drama and its quiet beauty, its chaos and its calm. I realized that what makes this place so special isn't just its landscapes or its wildlife; it's the way it makes you feel—alive, humbled, and connected.

Some journeys stay with you long after your bags are unpacked. Comoros, for me, will always be one of them.

EPILOGUE

If adventure does not run in your veins, you are tethered to the earth by fear.

– Freya Stark

What keeps us anchored to the ground when every part of us wants to soar? The answer isn't as simple as fear. Sometimes, it's love—love for the life we've built, the people we hold close, the stories we've already written. Other times, it's tradition, expectation, or the quiet hum of comfort. For me, it was a mix of all these things, woven into the fabric of a life that looked perfect from the outside.

Growing up as a third-culture child, my world was never small. My parents' home, alive with debates about gender, politics, and identity, taught me early to embrace difference. My mother, a feminist with unapologetic opinions, showed me the power of questioning. My father, her equal in every way, championed my independence. "The world is yours to explore," he'd tell me, his words like an open door I wasn't yet brave enough to walk through. Even with that foundation, my choices often felt weighed down by expectation—external, yes, but also internal. I wasn't just worried about disappointing others; I was terrified of failing myself. How do you let go of a life that's good in search of something that might be great? The question stayed with me for years until it became a whisper too loud to ignore: *Why not?*

A Gilded Cage

The comfort zone has a seductive allure. It's not a villain in our stories but a sanctuary. It's where the world feels safe and manageable, a place where risks are low, and outcomes are predictable. For me, it was a life filled with love, success, and stability—a life I'd built with my partner, Anand, across continents and against odds. But comfort can become a gilded cage. It's like standing in a room with beautiful walls but no windows. The longer you stay, the harder it is to leave, even as you begin to wonder what lies beyond. I loved the life I had, but a part of me was suffocating.

This isn't to say I leapt into the unknown without hesitation. Far from it. I wrestled with fear and doubt every step of the way. What if I failed? What if the world wasn't as welcoming as I hoped? What if I discovered that the path I was chasing led nowhere? But every time fear gripped me, that quiet mantra would rise in my mind: *Why not?*

Taking risks wasn't new to me. My life is shaped by decisions that others might have called bold, starting with the kind of marriage I share with Anand, a partnership built on mutual respect and shared adventure. From the start, we refused to let traditional roles define us. When I earned more than him in the early days of our marriage, there was no ego, no tension—only pride and encouragement.

It was Anand who pushed me to follow my instincts, even when it meant uprooting our lives. "You're not going to compromise on what you want," he told me when I hesitated to leave the U.S. for fear of starting over. And so we moved, together, into the unknown. But this chapter isn't about the risks we took as a couple—it's about the risks I took as an individual. It's about the times I handed over my passport at border crossings, trusting that the strangers holding it would see me as human and not as a threat. It's about navigating a cyclone in Malawi with my mother by my side, her faith in me stronger than my own. It's about walking into war-torn cities like Kabul and Damascus, places the world had labeled dangerous, and finding kindness, resilience, and connection.

Fear was always with me on these journeys, but it wasn't a barrier—it was a companion. I learned to carry it with me, to let it sit in the passenger seat without ever letting it take the wheel.

The True Courage... is Vulnerability

The world often mistakes confidence for invulnerability, but the truth is, my travels have been shaped by vulnerability at every turn. Trusting a guide in Afghanistan, listening to the stories of survivors in Syria, or simply navigating a language I didn't speak—all of these moments demanded a willingness to be vulnerable. And vulnerability, I've learned, isn't weakness. It's the foundation of courage. It's what allows us to connect with others, to grow, to discover who we are. Every time I stepped into the unknown, I found not just resilience but also humanity—the kind of humanity that bridges divides and defies stereotypes.

This question—so small yet so powerful—has become the heartbeat of my life. It's the question that carried me out of my comfort zone and into the world. It's the question that turned fear into curiosity and vulnerability into strength. But this isn't just my question; it's yours too. *Why not?* Why not take the first step, even if it's small? Why not risk failure for the chance of something extraordinary? Why not trust yourself to navigate the unknown?

The world is vast, yes, but it's also waiting. It's waiting for you to ask the hard questions, to take the bold steps, to discover the stories only you can tell. And trust me, the moment you let go of the ground and take flight, you'll wonder why you ever hesitated. Because life isn't measured by the walls you build around you but by the horizons you dare to chase. And every horizon, no matter how far, begins with a single question: *Why not?*

Reflecting on the journeys that have shaped me, I don't write as an expert or as someone with all the answers. I write as someone who has wrestled with fear, made countless mistakes, and stumbled into wisdom only after the fact. If my experiences resonate, it's not because I've done something extraordinary but because I've learned, step by step, that the extraordinary lies within reach of us all. I've been where you are—safe within the familiar, questioning whether stepping beyond it is worth the risk. My comfort zone wasn't the absence of adventure but the habit of sticking to the expected. For years, my travel choices mirrored my life: calculated, curated, and, in hindsight, somewhat unremarkable. Even as I longed for more, I hesitated, bound by invisible constraints of expectation and fear.

My Silent Teacher

I vividly remember the moment I realized my comfort zone wasn't just a safe haven—it was also a prison. It was a routine trip with friends to a well-known destination. Everything was predictable: the itinerary, the conversations, even the emotions I was supposed to feel. At some point, surrounded by breathtaking landscapes, I caught myself going through the motions. I wasn't moved; I was merely checking boxes.

That realization stung. If the joy of discovery could feel this hollow, I wondered, was it because I wasn't really discovering anything? My trips had become extensions of my daily life, comfortable but uninspired. The thought stayed with me, gnawing at the edges of my mind, until I finally asked the question that would change everything: *What am I so afraid of?* The answer, I realized, wasn't dramatic. It was a mix of small fears—fear of failure, of judgment, of discomfort. None of them seemed insurmountable, but together, they had kept me rooted in place.

The first time I consciously stepped beyond my comfort zone, it wasn't a glamorous, Instagram-worthy moment. It was a solo trip to a city I'd never been to before, one not far from where I lived. It felt insignificant, almost trivial, yet it terrified me. I fretted over everything: where I would eat, how I would navigate, whether I'd feel awkward being alone. And then, something incredible happened. I got lost. Not in a metaphorical sense but in a very literal one, wandering through streets I didn't recognize, surrounded by signs I couldn't read. My heart raced with panic, but amidst the anxiety, I found something unexpected—a deep sense of capability. I asked for help, found my way, and even stumbled upon a tiny café that served the most unforgettable meal of my life.

That experience taught me something I carry to this day: fear isn't the enemy; it's a doorway. Every time I've faced it, I've come out stronger, more confident, and more curious about what else the world has to offer. As a woman, and particularly as an Indian woman, stepping out into the world alone came with its own unique challenges. The societal narrative was loud and clear: the world is dangerous, especially for you. Every decision I made—to travel solo, to visit places off the beaten path, to trust strangers—felt like a small rebellion.

I share these stories not to say, "Look what I've done," but to say, "This is what I've learned." Every misstep, every moment of fear, and every triumph has given me a deeper understanding of myself and the world. When I talk about empowerment, it's not in abstract terms. It's the practical, messy, and deeply personal work of facing fears one at a time. It's learning to trust yourself in unfamiliar environments, whether that's a remote village in Southeast Asia or a crowded train station in Europe. Travel has taught me that empowerment isn't a destination; it's a process. It's built in moments of uncertainty when you figure out how to read a map in a foreign language or summon the courage to strike up a conversation with a stranger. These moments, small as they may seem, accumulate into something transformative.

Why I Share

If I sound passionate, it's because I know the impact this journey has had on me, and I want others to experience it too. But I also know that every person's path will look different. What matters isn't the scale of the adventure but the willingness to take that first step, however small it might be.

So, as you read this, I encourage you not to measure yourself against anyone else's story. Instead, look inward. What are the small, quiet fears holding you back? What's the one step you could take today to challenge them? The answers won't come all at once, and they won't be easy. But if there's one thing I've learned, it's that the discomfort of stepping into the unknown is far outweighed by the joy of discovering who you are on the other side.

And if you're wondering where to start, maybe begin with the question that changed everything for me: *Why not?*

Solutions for Safe and Empowering Travel

Travel is as much about preparation as it is about discovery, especially when navigating the unique challenges faced by women. Over years of exploration—sometimes joyful, sometimes nerve-wracking—I've learned that equipping yourself with the right tools and mindset can turn challenges into opportunities and fears into strengths. These strategies, born of experience, have not only helped me navigate unfamiliar places but also deepened my appreciation for the incredible diversity of our world.

1. Technology: Your Modern-Day Compass

In the digital age, your smartphone is a traveler's Swiss Army knife. Beyond the basics like navigation and communication, a simple language translator app can be a game-changer:

- **Navigation:** Apps like Google Maps and Maps.me are lifesavers. Before heading out, download offline maps so you're never caught without directions.
- **Language Translator:** Apps such as Google Translate or iTranslate can break down language barriers in moments. On a trip to Japan, this feature saved me when I found myself in a rural town trying to navigate a train schedule written entirely in Kanji. A quick photo using Google Translate turned a potentially stressful moment into a seamless journey.
- **Emergency Contact:** Stay connected with WhatsApp or Telegram to share live locations and stay in touch with loved ones. It's a comfort to know that even if you're across the globe, someone always knows where you are.

Before departing, preload your phone with local emergency numbers, embassy contacts, and screenshots of critical travel details. These little steps can save precious time in unexpected situations.

2. Building Networks: The Power of Community

Traveling alone doesn't mean traveling disconnected. Over the years, I've discovered how transformative it can be to connect with others:

- **Online Communities:** Platforms like Reddit's r/solotravel, Facebook groups (*Women Who Travel* or *Indian Wanderers*), and Couchsurfing forums provide invaluable tips and camaraderie.
- **Local Connections:** I remember visiting Istanbul and striking up a conversation with a fellow traveler I'd met through a travel group. That connection led to an unforgettable day exploring hidden corners of the city I might never have found on my own.

The friendships and advice you gain from these networks don't just enrich your travels—they remind you that the world is full of people willing to share their stories, support, and kindness.

3. Situational Awareness: A Seasoned Traveler's Intuition

Situational awareness is a skill that grows with experience. In every destination, understanding the nuances of culture, customs, and geography is as essential as packing your passport.

- **Blend In:** Dress appropriately for the culture you're visiting, not only to show respect but also to avoid standing out unnecessarily. I learned this lesson the hard way on a trip to Jordan, where adjusting to local norms made interactions more comfortable and enjoyable.

- **Pre-Trip Research:** Before arriving, familiarize yourself with customs that could impact your safety or experience. Knowing, for example, that certain gestures might be offensive or which areas to avoid at night can make a significant difference.

- **Stay Alert:** Trust your instincts. If something feels off—a deserted street, persistent attention, or a dubious situation—don't hesitate to change your plans or ask for help.

4. Finding and Working with Local Guides

The right local guide can transform a trip into a deeper cultural exchange, opening doors to experiences most travelers miss:

- **Use Trusted Platforms:** Websites like ToursByLocals or GetYourGuide are invaluable for finding vetted guides.

- **Ask the Right Questions:** On a trip to Morocco, I reached out to a guide in advance, asking about their experience with solo female travelers. Their thoughtful responses reassured me and made the trip a highlight of my journey.

- **Verify Through Reviews:** Reading feedback from fellow travelers, especially women, can provide insight into the guide's professionalism and understanding of cultural nuances.

5. Navigating Complicated Destinations

Some places require more planning than others, but that doesn't mean they should be avoided:

- **Plan Strategically:** In Afghanistan, I found that having a detailed itinerary paired with flexibility helped me adapt to unexpected changes while still feeling in control.

- **Daylight Travel:** I've learned the importance of arriving at destinations during daylight hours. One arrival in Ethiopia after sunset taught me how unsettling it can be to navigate unfamiliar streets in the dark. Since then, I've prioritized timing for peace of mind.

- **Dress Modestly and Mindfully:** In countries like Iran, adhering to local dress codes not only enhanced my safety but also allowed me to connect more authentically with locals who appreciated the gesture of respect.

6. Overcoming Language Barriers

A single word can open doors, and a smile paired with a simple "hello" in the local language can create connections that transcend cultural divides. Language apps make it easier than ever:

- **Text-to-Speech Features:** On a trip to Vietnam, I used Google Translate to negotiate with a vendor in a bustling market. What started as a transactional conversation quickly turned into shared laughter over mangled pronunciations, creating a memorable moment of connection.

- **Learn a Few Phrases:** Knowing basic words like "thank you," "please," and "help" can make a significant impact. Locals often respond warmly to even the clumsiest attempts at their language.

7. Practical Tips for Visa Hurdles

Indian travelers know the complexities of visa applications all too well, but patience and preparation can ease the process:

- **Start Early:** Research visa requirements as soon as you've chosen your destination. Processing times can vary widely, and having everything in order reduces last-minute stress.

- **Seek Help if Needed:** Professional visa services or experienced travel agents can be invaluable, especially for destinations with intricate requirements.

- **Have Backup Plans:** During a trip to Europe, a delayed Schengen visa taught me the importance of flexibility. I rerouted through a country with visa-on-arrival access, turning an obstacle into an unexpected adventure.

Lessons from the Road

Every strategy I've shared comes from lived experience. From navigating rural train schedules in Japan with a translation app to improvising plans when flights were canceled in Comoros, each challenge has been a stepping stone toward confidence.

Traveling isn't about eliminating risks but learning to manage them. The more you prepare, the more you'll trust yourself to handle the unexpected—and the more empowered you'll feel to embrace the extraordinary.

So, as you set out on your own journeys, remember that the world is vast, welcoming, and waiting for you. Equip yourself with these tools, trust in your resourcefulness, and take that first step boldly. Because every great adventure begins with the courage to try.

The Real Hustle: Traveling with a Full-Time Job

Let's get one thing straight—despite what Instagram might have you believe, you don't need to quit your job and become a full-time traveler to explore the world. Trust me, I know this because I've done it differently. I never dropped everything for a nomadic life. Instead, I made my career and my wanderlust work together, weaving them into a rhythm that lets me experience the best of both worlds.

Balancing a full-time job with an unrelenting desire to see the world isn't easy, but it's far from impossible. It requires discipline, foresight, and a touch of audacity. Over the years, I've honed a system that keeps my career thriving while still leaving room for new adventures. If anything, this balance has made my travels even more meaningful, knowing I've earned every mile along the way.

Mastering the Art of Planning

If there's one secret to making it all work, it's meticulous planning. Every January, I sit down with a calendar and map out my year, trip by trip. National holidays, long weekends, and a sprinkling of half-days become the foundation for my travel plans. By blocking off these windows early, I turn them into opportunities: a week in South America here, a long weekend in Georgia (the country, not the state) there.

One of my most fulfilling trips—a six-day whirlwind trek through Honduras—came from carefully piecing together vacation days around a public holiday. Another time, a four-day jaunt to Kenya let me witness the Great Migration without sacrificing work commitments. This kind of strategy allows me to plan big-ticket trips months in advance, secure the best deals, and stay ahead of visa hurdles.

Sunday mornings are sacred for travel logistics. With my laptop open and a filter coffee in hand, I delve into research. Page five of Google, niche forums, and hidden corners of Tripadvisor are where I find the real gems. Whether it's securing a fixer in Afghanistan who navigated delicate political landscapes or connecting with a baker in South Sudan who shared her recipe for roadside chapati, the details matter. The relationships I've built through this meticulous groundwork have added depth and meaning to my journeys, reminding me that the best adventures often lie far from the obvious path.

Let's face it—no matter how much you love traveling, a toxic workplace can crush your energy and leave you with no bandwidth to plan or enjoy your trips. I've been fortunate to work for a boss who values what travel brings to my life, understanding that it's more than a hobby—it's a source of growth and perspective. . I have already spoken about my awesome feminist boss earlier in the book. But let me be clear: finding such a workplace wasn't luck; it was intention. From the outset, I sought roles where I could communicate openly about my interests and negotiate time off without guilt. I've learned to be upfront about my boundaries, and I advocate for myself when it comes to managing workload before and after a trip. If you're stuck in a job that drains you, start by carving out small wins. Advocate for your time, set non-negotiables around personal commitments, and work toward building a career that values you as a whole person, not just as a worker.

Travel doesn't have to mean weeks-long escapades or quitting everything for a year-long sabbatical. Some of my most memorable experiences have come from trips lasting less than a week. The key is to be intentional and let go of the pressure to "see it all."

Take my trip to Jordan, for example. In just five days, I visited Petra, floated in the Dead Sea, and explored Amman's vibrant streets. By focusing on a few meaningful experiences instead of cramming in every landmark, I found moments that stayed with me far longer than a rushed itinerary ever could.

Remember, it's not about the quantity of time you spend in a place but the quality of the moments you experience. Be present, engage deeply, and savor what you can—whether it's a simple conversation with a local elder or the way the light filters through an unlisted canyon hike.

One of the biggest myths about travel is that it requires an overflowing bank account. It doesn't—it requires priority. My husband and I have a travel fund that automatically siphons a portion of our income each month. It's a non-negotiable part of our budget, much like rent or utilities. We've also learned to resist lifestyle inflation. Fancy gadgets, excessive dining out, and impulse purchases have taken a backseat to the thrill of planning our next adventure. Saving becomes less about sacrifice and more about building toward something extraordinary.

The Passport Problem

As an Indian traveler, visas are an unavoidable part of the hustle. Yes, they're time-consuming, frustrating, and sometimes demoralizing. I've faced rejections, missed out on opportunities, and endured endless paperwork, but I've also discovered incredible destinations I might never have considered otherwise. Instead of following the crowd to over-Instagrammed locations, I've made a habit of exploring places that are easier to access with my passport. From the surreal landscapes of Botswana to the bustling charm of Cambaodia, these "offbeat" destinations have rewarded me with unforgettable experiences.

Traveling with a full-time job isn't a pipe dream—it's a puzzle. It takes effort, patience, and a willingness to prioritize, but the rewards are immeasurable. There will be hurdles—unexpected projects, dwindling savings, or visa complications—but don't lose sight of why you started. For me, the joy of discovering the world while holding onto a career I love is worth every ounce of effort. The secret isn't about having unlimited time or money; it's about determination and smart planning. So, plan, hustle, and take those small, meaningful steps. And remember: You don't need to choose between your career and your wanderlust. With a little creativity and a lot of heart, you can have both.

Finding Home in the World

Maya Angelou said, *"The ache for home lives in all of us, the safe place where we can go as we are and not be questioned."* As I write these final words, the weight of this journey settles in—a journey that spans not just 104 countries but countless moments of discovery, resilience, and connection. The world has taught me something profound: that home is not defined by coordinates or walls but by the humanity we encounter and the emotions we allow ourselves to feel. In the end, the stamps on my passport are a beautiful collection, but they are only the surface. The real journey has been inward, unraveling layers of who I thought I was to discover the person I was becoming. Every meal shared with strangers, every story exchanged across cultural divides, every quiet moment under a foreign sky has stitched together the fabric of my understanding of what it means to belong.

In a quiet village in Congo, I found home in the laughter of a family who had little but gave me everything. Around a modest dinner table, we shared stories and rice, and in those moments, I was no longer a stranger but one of them. In Syria, amid a landscape marked by hardship, I found home in the kindness of locals who invited me into their lives. Over meals seasoned with stories of resilience and hope, I understood the strength of human connection.

Home, I've come to realize, is not a place. It's a feeling—a thread of warmth, understanding, and belonging that ties us to one another no matter where we are. It's in the hands that pass you a plate of food, in the unspoken kindness of a stranger who helps you find your way, in the stories that turn acquaintances into friends.

A Universal Truth

Travel has revealed something universal: wherever I've been, from the deserts of Algeria to the fjords of Norway, people share the same desires. We all yearn for connection, understanding, and a sense of community. The language may change, the customs may differ, but the heart of it all remains the same.

That truth has been my constant, a quiet reassurance as I moved through the unfamiliar. It's why I've never felt truly lost, no matter how far I've wandered. Because home isn't where you come from—it's what you carry with you and create along the way.

Now, dear reader, the baton passes to you. What will your journey look like? Where will you find your sense of belonging? It doesn't have to involve planes or passports. Home might be waiting in the people you surround yourself with, in the passions you nurture, or in the risks you've yet to take. Ask yourself: what fills your soul with peace? What connections ignite a sense of purpose within you? And more importantly, what's stopping you from pursuing them?

This book isn't an instruction manual. It's an invitation—an open door to a world of infinite possibilities. Whether your path leads you to a bustling city, a quiet mountainside, or a new relationship with yourself, let it be one you choose with intention and courage.

Why Not?

As I close this chapter and this book, I leave you with the question that has guided my life: *Why not?* Why not challenge the limits of what you believe is possible? Why not trust in the kindness of strangers? Why not embrace the uncertainty that comes with chasing your dreams?

Travel has taught me that the greatest rewards lie beyond our comfort zones. It has shown me that fear is not the enemy; stagnation is. It has proven that even the smallest steps can lead to the most transformative journeys.

So here's my hope for you: that you take that first step. That you embrace the hustle, the beauty, and the mess of life as it unfolds. That you find joy not in ticking off destinations but in savoring the moments that take your breath away. That you choose connection over perfection, curiosity over judgment, and courage over hesitation. The world is waiting. Your story is waiting. And home? It's wherever you decide to make it. Go forth boldly, live fully, and remember: the question isn't whether you can—it's whether you'll dare to ask yourself, *Why not?*

With all my love,

Ankitha Rajendaran